A Glimpse at the
Beauty of Islam

Prepared by

Darussalam Research Division

DARUSSALAM

DARUSSALAM
GLOBAL LEADER IN ISLAMIC BOOKS
Riyadh · Jeddah · Al-Khober · Sharjah
Lahore · London · Houston · New York

First Edition: August 2001

Supervised by:

ABDUL MALIK MUJAHID

Headquarters:

P.O. Box: 22743, Riyadh 11416, KSA
Tel: 00966-1-4033962/4043432
Fax:00966-1- 4021659
E-mail: darussalam@naseej.com.sa
Website: http:// www.dar-us-salam.com
Bookshop: Tel & Fax: 00966-1-4614483

Branches & Agents:

K.S. A.

● Jeddah: Tel & Fax: 00966-2-6807752
● Al-Khobar: Tel & Fax: 00966-3-8692900

U.A.E.

● Tel: 00971-6-5511293 Fax: 5511294

PAKISTAN

● 50 Lower Mall, Lahore
   Tel: 0092-42-724 0024 Fax: 7354072

● Rahman Market, Ghazni Street
   Urdu Bazar, Lahore
   Tel: 0092-42-7120054 Fax: 7320703

U. S. A.

● Houston: P.O. Box: 79194 Tx 77279
   Tel: 001-713-722 0419 Fax: 001-713-722 0431
   E-mail: Sales @ dar-us-salam.com
   Website: http:// www.dar-us-salam.com

● New York: 572 Atlantic Ave, Brooklyn
   New York-11217
   Tel: 001-718-625 5925

U.K.

● London: Darussalam International Publications Ltd.
   226 High Street, Walthamstow, London E17 7JH U.K.
   Tel: 0044-208 520 2666 Mobile: 0044-794 730 6706
   Fax: 0044-208 521 7645
● Darussalam International Publications Limited
   Regent Park Mosque, 146 Park Road, London Nw8 7RG
   Tel: 0044-207 724 3363

AUSTRALIA

● Lakemba NSW: ICIS: Ground Floor 165-171, Haldon St.
   Tel: (61-2) 9758 4040 Fax: 9758 4030

MALAYSIA

● E&D BOOKS SDN.BHD.-321 B 3rd Floor, Suria Klcc
   Kuala Lumpur City Center 50088
   Tel: 00603-21663433 Fax: 459 72032

SINGAPORE

● Muslim Converts Association of Singapore
   Singapore- 424484
   Tel: 0065-440 6924, 348 8344 Fax: 440 6724

SRI LANKA

● Darul Kitab 6, Nirmal Road, Colombo-4
   Tel: 0094-1-589 038 Fax: 0094-74 722433

KUWAIT

● Islam Presentation Committee
   Enlightment Book Shop
   P.O. Box : 1613, Safat 13017 KUWAIT
   Tel: 00965-244 7526, Fax: 240 0057

BANGLADESH

● 30 Malitola Road, Dhaka-1100
   Tel: 0088-02-9557214, Fax: 0088-02-9559738

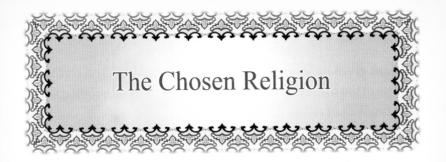

The Chosen Religion

Allâh the All-Mighty says:

"This day have I perfected your religion for you and completed My favor upon you and have chosen for you Islam as your religion." (5:3)

This was the last Verse revealed chronologically to Prophet Muhammed ﷺ. Making the completion of the Qur'ân and the perfection of Islam. Islam is complete and perfect and is not thereafter susceptible to addition or abrogation. Being eternal and universal, the Islamic Law, which was made by God [Allâh] Himself Who knows what is best for us under all circumstances, is resilient and adjustable to the changing conditions of time and place. The perfection of Islam is manifest in the fact that God [Allâh] has made it reign supreme and prevail over other religions. God's favor upon the Muslims is manifest in the fact that He granted them true guidance, support and honor in this world and in the Hereafter. He has also chosen for them Islam as their religion because it is the Truth, and for this reason He will not accept any other religion but Islam.

"And whoever seeks a religion other than Islam, it shall not be accepted from him, and in the life to come he shall be among the losers." (3:58)

The Chosen Religion

Islam gives its followers happiness in this world and eternal bliss in the life to come. Islam simply means total submission to the Will of Allâh. Therefore, it is the same in essence, whether given to Noah, Abraham, Moses, Jesus or to Muhammad. For the message it calls to is the same, and the source of unity is the revelation from Allâh:

"He has ordained for you the same religion [Islam] which He enjoined on Noah, and that which We have revealed to you, and which We enjoined on Abraham, Moses and Jesus: namely that you should remain steadfast in religion and be not divided therein." (42:13)

After the corruption of the older Scriptures, the Qur'ân came with a twofold purpose: first to confirm the true and original message, namely that of Islam, and second to stand as a witness to it by confirming the truth and rejecting the falsehood which over time came into the older Scriptures. Muslims are required to believe in these Scriptures and to make no distinction between any of them or the Messengers who brought them because they all come from the One True God:

"Say [O Muhammad to the Jews and Christians], 'We believe in Allâh and that which has been sent to us and

that which has been sent down to Abraham, Ishmael, Isaac, Jacob and to *Al-Asbât*, [1] and that which has been given to Moses and Jesus, and that which has been given to the Prophets from their Lord. We make no distinction between any of them, and to Him we have submitted [in Islam]." (2:136)

Some of these Scriptures are still existent but not in their original form as a result of the human omissions and additions that have crept into them. The Qur'ân is the only Divine Scripture which has stood the test of time without any change because it is the Truth from God [Allâh], and the Truth never fades or diminishes:

"That which We have revealed to you [O Muhammad 襲] of the Book [i.e., the Qur'ân] is the Truth, confirming that which was [revealed] before it." (35:31)

The truth contained in the Qur'ân will never be compromised because Allâh has taken upon Himself the responsibility of preserving it:

"Verily We have sent the Reminder (i.e., the Qur'ân), and We will assuredly guard it [from corruption]." (15:9)

"Verily, it is an honorable well-fortified book of exalted power [because it is Allâh's Speech, and He

---

1   *Al-Asbât* refers to the offspring of the twelve sons of Jacob.

The Chosen Religion

has protected it from corruption]. No falsehood can approch it from before or after it: it is set down by the All-Wise, Worthy of all praise." (41:41-2)

The revealed Scriptures before the advent of Prophet Muhammad ﷺ, such as the Old Testament and the Gospel, were written long after the demise of the Prophets to whom they were revealed. The entire Qur'ân on the contrary, was completely written in the lifetime of the Prophet ﷺ on such things as pieces of palm trees, parchments and bones. Besides, tens of thousands of the Prophet's Companions committed it to memory while it was being revealed. The Qur'ân is still memorized and read in its original language, Arabic, and taught to millions of people the world over. In fact, with every succeeding generation of Muslims, the number of those who have committed the entire Qur'ân to memory has increased incredibly. There is no other book, religious or otherwise, which has been given this unparalleled care in recorded history.

The eternal care with which the unadulterated teachings of Islam have been authentically recorded and preserved throughout the ages is a clear evidence of the universality of the message of Islam and the finality of the Prophethood of the Prophet Muhammad ﷺ. The Qur'ân is now available in its original form without change of any kind. The perfect preservation of the Qur'ân signifies the preservation of Islam. That is why Allâh says in the Qur'ân:

"Verily the only acceptable religion to Allâh is Islam." (3:19)

The Chosen Religion

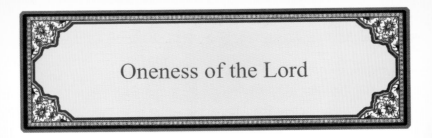

Oneness of the Lord

Islam calls to the belief that the Creator of the universe is One and Unique without any partners. His nature is so sublime that it is far beyond our limited conceptions. He is not a mere abstract of philosophy. All the creatures testify to His Existence, and none are comparable to Him. The unity of design and that of the fundamental facts of creation and existence of the universe proclaim His Oneness. He is the Eternal, without beginning or end, the Absolute, Who is not limited by time or place or circumstance. He is the Creator, the Sustainer and the Planner of the whole universe. None has the right to be worshipped except Him. He has the Most Beautiful Names and the Loftiest Attributes. His Knowledge extends to everything seen and unseen, present and future, near and far. His Grace and Mercy are unbounded. He is the All-Mighty, the All-Wise:

> "Say: 'He is Allâh, the One; Allâh, the Eternal, Absolute; He begets not, nor is He begotten; and there is none equal or comparable to him.'"(112:1-4)

> "There is nothing whatever like unto Him, and He is the All-Hearing, the All-Seeing."(42:11)

> "He is the First [nothing is before Him], the Last [nothing is after Him], the Most High [nothing is above Him] and the Most Near [nothing is nearer then Him].

And he has full knowledge of all things." (57:3)

"He is Allâh, besides Whom none has the right to be worshipped, the All-Knower of the unseen and the seen. He is the Most Gracious, the Most Merciful. He is Allâh besides Whom none has the right to be worshipped, the King, the Holy, the One Free from all defects, the Giver of security, the Watcher over His creatures, the All-Mighty, the Compeller, the Supreme. Glory be to Allâh! [High is He] above what they associate as partners with Him. He is Allâh, the Creator, the Inventor of all things the Bestower of forms. To Him belong the Best Names. All that is in the heavens and the earth glorify Him. And he is All-Mighty, the All-Wise." (59:23-4)

"And they attribute falsely without knowledge sons and daughters to Him. Be He Glorified! [For He is] above what they attribute to Him! He is the Originator of the heavens and the earth. How can He have a son when He has no wife? He created all things, and He has full knowledge of everything. Such is Allâh, your Lord! None has the right to be worshipped but He, the Creator of all things. So worship Him [Alone]. And He has the power to dispose of all affairs. No vision can grasp Him, but His Grasp is over all vision. He is the Most Subtle, Well-Aware." (6:100-3)

Tauhîd or monotheism constitutes the essence of the teachings of Islam. It signifies that there is One Supreme Lord of the universe. He is the Omnipotent and the Sustainer

of the world and mankind. Unity pervades the whole universe. All of Allâh's creatures testify to His Oneness. This can be seen in their utter submission to His Will. The perpetual succession of day and night in the most orderly manner; the course of the sun, the moon and the mighty stars; the ceaseless alternation of the four seasons; the functioning of the whole universe including its most subtle elements in the most precise and systematic manner. In fact the great marvels and the impressive wonders of the universe are like open books which tell us about the Wisdom, Power, Greatness and Divine skill of this Great Artist Who is Allâh.

Oneness of the Lord

Some Signs to Ponder about

How can one observe the inexhaustible creativity of nature, its purposefulness, its preservation of the morally useful and destruction of the socially injurious, and yet fail to draw the conclusion that behind nature there is an all-pervading mind. A mind whose ceaseless creative activity the processes of nature - is but an outward manifestation! The stars scattered through infinite space, the vast panorama of nature with its charm and beauty, the regular waxing and waning of the moon, the astonishing harmony of the seasons and the days and nights, the incessant supply of water, the delicate flowers and crystals beneath our feet - all point towards one fact: there is a God, the Creator, the Governor. We witness a superbly flawless plan in the universe; can it be without a Planner? We see overwhelming beauty and harmony in its working, can they be without a Creator? We observe beautiful intricate designs in nature; can it be without a Designer? We feel a lofty purpose in physical and human existence; can it be without a Will working behind it? We find that the universe is like a superbly written, fascinating adventure, can it be without an Author? Truly, God said:

"O mankind: worship your Lord, Who created you and those before you so that you may become righteous. Who has made the earth a resting place for you and the sky a canopy and sent down rain from the heavens, and

brought forth therewith fruits for your sustenance. Then do not set up rivals unto Allâh while you know [the truth]." (2:21-3)[1]

Allâh has the total might, the absolute will and complete perfect knowledge. He has provided human beings with all the necessary proofs in the universe and within themselves so that it becomes manifest to them that He is the true God, and therefore they should worship Him and discharge their duty towards Him in the best possible manner.

His signs are scattered everywhere, within ourselves and in the entire universe. He encourages us in many Verses of the Qur'ân to utilize our power of reasoning so that we can understand His Greatness and Wisdom. Sometimes He draws our attention to the Principle of Causality, which He established in the universe:

"Were they created of nothing, or were they themselves the creators?"(52:35)

This Verse clearly disproves beyond any shadow of doubt the baseless claims that man is created out of nothing or that he is his own creator.

Even people without any formal education at all recognize the principle that anything in the world has a Maker. A bedouin who lived in the heart of the desert was once asked: "What is your evidence of the existence of Allâh?" He replied, "Droppings are made by the camel the footprints

Some Signs to Ponder about

---

1   Khurshid Ahmad, Islam: Basic Principles and Characteristics, Islamic
     Foundation, Leicester, U.K., 1974. p.6. (With some editing.)

made by the feet. What about the sky and its mighty constellations, the mountains and their passes and the oceans and their great waves, do these not testify to the existence of the Omnipotent, Wise God?"

At other times He invites us to contemplate about the wonders of the heavens and the earth:

"Were they created by nothing or were they themselves the creators? Or did they create the heavens and the earth? Nay, they have no firm belief." (52:35-6)

"Say: 'Behold all that is in the heavens and on earth,' but neither signs nor warners benefit those who believe not." (10:101)

These Verses suggest that it is through the observation of the wonderfully designed creation in the heavens and the earth that we can understand the greatness and wisdom of the Creator. If, however, we let the innate faculties of observation, understanding and faith die, Allâh's signs in His creation or in the spoken word which His Messengers strove hard to convey, will never reach us any more than speech reaches a deaf person.

At other times He introduces the faculty of the intellect and insight into the amazing creation of the heavens and the marvelous objects they contain:

 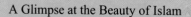

"Blessed is He Who has made constellations in the skies, and placed therein a lamp [i.e., the sun] and a moon giving light." (25:61)

"It is He Who made the sun radiate a brilliant light and the moon reflect a luster, and ordained for it stages, that you might know the number of years and the reckoning of time." (10:5)

"He causes the break of day; and He made the night for rest and the sun and the moon for reckoning." (6:96)

"Have they not looked at the sky above them, how We have made it and adorned it, and there are no flaws in it?" (50:6)

"And have they not looked into the kingdom of the heavens and the earth, and all things that Allâh has created?" (7:185)

"[It is He] Who has created seven heavens one above another. No incongruity can you see in the creation of the Most Beneficent. Then look again: Can you see any rifts? Again turn your vision a second time: your sight will [only] return to you confused and fatigued." (67:3-4)

The last Verse makes it obvious that Allâh's creation as represented in the visible world is flawless no matter how closely we observe it. We will find no flaw in Allâh's handiwork. It is our powers that we shall find fail to go beyond a certain limit. This Verse, as well as others, also invites us to study and observe the external world as minutely as our powers will allow.

Some Signs to Ponder about

At certain times He calls our attention to ponder on the earth and the various plants it contains:

> "And in the earth are diverse tracts, adjoining one another, and gardens of vines and fields sown with corn and palm trees, growing out of single roots or otherwise; they are watered with the same water, yet some of them We make more excellent than others to eat. Therein, verily, are signs for a people who understand." (13:4)

We can see plants of different and the same kinds which are all fed by the same kind of water, yet the fruit they yield is totally different from one another in taste, color and smell!

> "In this, verily, there is a sign." (26:67)

In some other contexts He invites us to reflect on water which He sends down from the sky, and which if it was His Will, He could have make it bitter and undrinkable!

> "And We send down water from the sky according to [due] measure, and We cause it to soak in the soil; and We certainly are able to drain it off [with ease]." (23:18)

Sometimes He points out His Oneness and peerless management and disposal of the affairs of the whole universe. Considering the unity of design and purpose in this wonderful universe of ours, a multiplicity of gods is intellectually indefensible:

> "Allâh has not taken unto Himself any son, nor is there

any other god along with Him; in that case each god would have taken away what he has created, and some of them would surely have dominated over others. Glorified be Allâh above all that which they attribute to Him!" (23:91)

Another Verse eloquently states:

"If there had been in them [i.e., the heavens and the earth] other gods besides Allâh, then surely both would have gone to ruin. Glorified then be Allâh, the Lord of the Throne, above what they attribute to Him!" (21:22)

Allâh's signs are everywhere. The Qur'ân is replete with beautiful descriptive Verses that call us to reflect on these magnificent, countless signs with the object of reaching the obvious fact of His existence. The Qur'ân says:

"Among His signs is this that He created you from dust; and then, behold, you are men acattered [far and wide]! And among His signs is this that He created for you mates from among yourselves, that you may dwell in tranquillity with them, and He has put love and mercy between your [hearts]. Verily in that are signs for those who reflect. And among His signs is the creation of the heavens and the earth, and the variations in your languages and your colors. Verily in that are signs for those who know. And among His signs is the sleep that you take by night and by day, and the quest that you make [for livelihood] out of His Bounty. Verily in that are signs for those who harken. And

Some Signs to Ponder about

among His signs, He shows you the lightening, by way both of fear and of hope, and He sends down rain from the sky and with it gives life to the earth after it is dead: Verily in that are signs for those who are wise. And among His signs is this that heaven and earth stand by His Command. Then when He calls you by a single call from the earth, behold, you [straightway] come forth. To Him belongs every being that is in the heavens and the earth. All are devoutly obedient to Him." (30:20-6)

"He created the heavens without any pillars that you can see; He set on the earth mountains standing firm, lest it should shake with you; and He scattered through it beasts of all kinds. We send down rain from the sky and produce on the earth every kind of noble creature, in pairs. Such is the creation of Allâh. Now show Me what is there that others besides Him have created. Nay, but the transgressors are in manifest error." (31:10-1)

"It is Allâh Who causes the seed grain and the date stone to split and sprout. He causes the living to issue from the dead. And He is the One to cause the dead to issue from the living. That is Allâh: then how are you deluded away from the truth? He it is that cleaves the daybreak [from the dark]. He makes the night for rest and tranquillity, and the sun and the moon for the reckoning [of time]: such is the judgment and ordering of [Him], the Exalted in Power, the Omniscient. It is

Some Signs to Ponder about

He Who makes the stars [as beacons] for you, that you may guide yourselves, with their help, through the dark spaces of land and sea. We detail Our signs for people who know. It is He Who has produced you from a single soul: then there is a resting place and a repository. We detail Our signs for people who understand. It is He Who sends down rain from the skies: with it We produce vegetation of all kinds: from some We produce green [crops], out of which We produce, close-compounded grain out of the date palm and its sheaths [of spates] [come] clusters of dates hanging low and near: and [then there are] gardens of grapes and olives, and pomegranates, each similar [in kind] yet different [in variety]: when they begin to bear fruit, feast your eyes with the fruit and the ripeness thereof. Behold! In these thing there are signs for people who believe." (6:95-99)

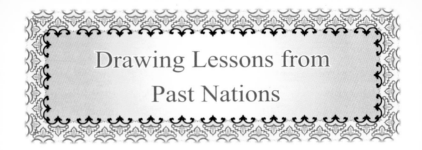

Drawing Lessons from Past Nations

The Qur'ân not only invites us to contemplate Allâh's signs but also to draw lessons from history by finding out about the end of past nations who rejected Faith and followed their whims and desires. It invites us to contemplate how the kingdoms and empires that were once flourishing brought about their own ruin as a result of their disobedience to the Law of Allâh:

"Do they not travel through the earth, and see what was the end of those before them [who did evil]? Allâh brought utter destruction upon them, and similar [fates await] those who reject Allâh." (47:10)

"Do they not travel through the earth, and see what was the end of those before them? They were superior to them in strength: they tilled the soil and populated it in greater numbers than these have done: there came to them their Messengers with clear signs [which they rejected to their own destruction]: it was not Allâh who wronged them, but they wronged their own souls." (30:9)

"Do they not travel through the land, so that their hearts [and minds] may thus learn wisdom and their ears may

thus learn to hear? Truly it is not the eyes that are blind, but the hearts which are in their breasts." (22:46)

"Does it not teach them a lesson, how many generations We destroyed before them, in whose dwellings they [now] walk about? Verily in that are signs. Would they not then listen?" (32:26)

One of the eye-opening stories that is repeatedly mentioned in the Qur'ân is that of Moses and Pharaoh. Pharaoh was a very stubborn and cruel oppressor who enslaved the Israelites and refused to accept the truth that Moses presented to him along with other numerous clear signs. His wealth and splendor was of no benefit to him when Allâh's Decree came to pass. The Qur'ân says of him when he was drowning in the Red Sea:

"This day shall we save you in your body, that you may be a sign to those who come after you! But verily, many among mankind are heedless of Our signs!" (10:92)

Drawing Lessons from Past Nations

It was Allâh's Will that the Pharaoh's earthly remains be preserved to be a sign to man. The material presence of the mummified body of the man who knew Moses and resisted his pleas is still with us.

The stories that the Qur'ân mentions, are not meant for entertainment but for reflection. The Qur'ân says:

"There is, in their stories, instruction for men endued with understanding." (12:111)

The Qur'ân instructs the Prophet ﷺ to relate these stories for the same purpose:

"So relate the stories; perchance they may reflect." (7:176)

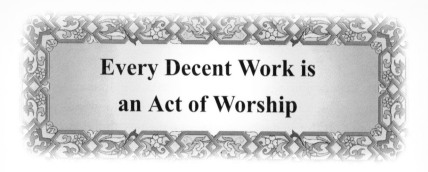

Every Decent Work is an Act of Worship

The world is an entity created by God [Allâh] for meaningful purposes. He has not created anything without a purpose:

"And We created not the heaven and earth and all that between them, without purpose!" (38:27)

Creation is not for idle sport or play, as the Qur'ân states in many Verses. Allâh has a serious purpose behind it:

"I have created not the jinn and mankind except that they should worship Me." (51:56)

This Verse indicates that God [Allâh] created human beings and the jinn in order to worship Him. Many people nowadays including some Muslims think that worship is limited to religious rituals only such as prayer, charity and fasting. This rather distorted meaning of worship has no place in Islam. Since the teachings of Islam encompass all aspects of life, all human acts are deemed acts of worship if they are done for Allâh alone and in accordance with His Divine Law and the teachings of His Last Messenger. Islam appreciates noble motives and honorable intentions behind all acts and abundantly rewards them. The Prophet ﷺ says:

"Actions are by intentions, and every person will have what he has intended." *(Al-Bukhârî and Muslim)*

The two conditions mentioned above are like a 'magic wand', which turns daily lawful practices into great acts of worship. If, for instance, one takes a meal with the intention of being in good health to better fulfil one's obligations towards Allâh, one's fellow human beings and oneself in the manner prescribed by Allâh, one will certainly receive a great reward for such a good intention.

Decent work, which does not involve forbidden activities like cheating and deceiving people, is an act of worship; eating and drinking with the intention to gain strength to worship Allâh better is an act of worship; even having intimate relations with one's wife is an act of worship. The Prophet ﷺ once told his Companions:

> "You will be rewarded even when you engage in sexual intercourse [with your wives]."

> Astonished, the Companions asked, "How can We get rewarded for satisfying our [sexual] desire?" The Prophet ﷺ asked them, "If you satisfy your desires unlawfully, will you be committing a sin for doing so?" They replied, "Yes." "Likewise," he said, "by satisfying it lawfully [with your wives] you will be rewarded for it." *(Muslim)*

Worship is all-inclusive and includes numerous things that many people mistakenly deem insignificant. The Prophet ﷺ says:

> "Receiving your [Muslim] brother with a smile is a form of charity, helping a person to load his animal is a

Every Decent Work is an Act of Worship

form of charity, and putting some water in your neighbor's bucket is a form of charity." *(Al-Bukhârî)*

"Do not consider any act of goodness insignificant, even if it is receiving your [Muslim] brother with a smile." *(Al-Bukhârî)*

"Every act of goodness is in fact an act of charity." *(Al-Bukhârî)*

In a nutshell, the concept of worship in Islam is all-inclusive so long as the two conditions mentioned above are met. This thought imbues a Muslim's heart with great joy when he realizes that all his actions are acts of worship. This very thought is bound to help a Muslim to carry out all actions conscientiously in order to win Allâh's Pleasure, whether he is alone or with his superiors because he knows that he is watched at all times by the One Who is the All-Watcher. Neither slumber nor sleep overtakes Him.

Every Decent Work is an Act of Worship

A Simple and Easy Religion

Islam is a very simple religion with a very clear and simple set of beliefs and practices. It is also a very easy religion. The Qur'ân says:

> "He [Allâh] has not laid upon you in religion any hardship." (22:78)

The Prophet ﷺ says:

> "This religion [of Islam] is very easy, and whoever overburdens himself in his religion will not be able to continue in that way. So you should not be extremists, but try to be near to perfection..." (Al-Bukhârî)

'Âishah رضي الله عنها the Prophet's wife said:

> "Whenever Allâh's Messenger ﷺ was given the opportunity to choose between two things, he would always choose the easier and the more convenient things." (Al-Bukhârî)

Islam assures its followers that Allâh will accept from them just such duty as they have the ability to offer. The Qur'ân says:

> "On no soul does Allâh place a burden greater than it can bear." (2:286)

Islam allows for the various circumstances one may encounter in one's life, and thus provides better and easier alternatives for its followers. To clarify this point we will consider two examples. *Salât* [prayer] in Islam is considered invalid without the performance of *Wudhu'* [ablution]. A Muslim is required to perform ablution by washing some parts of his or her body with water. This requirement, however, can under certain circumstances be substituted with *Tayammum,* or the wiping over the face and hands with clean dust, sand or earth. The Qur'ân says:

"O you who believe! When you intend to offer *Salât* [prayer], wash your faces and your hands [forearms] up to te elbows; rub [by passing wet hands over] your heads and [wash] your feet up to the ankles. If you are in a state of ceremonial impurity [as a result of sexual discharge], bathe your whole body. But if you are ill, or on a journey, or any of you comes from answering the call of nature, or you have been in contact with

A Simple and Easy Religion

women [i.e., sexual intercourse], and you find no water, then take for yourselves clean sand or earth, and rub therewith your faces and hands. Allâh does not wish to place you in a difficulty, but to make you clean, and to complete His favor to you, that you may be grateful." (5:6)

There is no need for making up for fasting if someone eats or drinks forgetfully or mistakenly or under threat or compulsion. Allâh says:

"But if one is forced by necessity, without willful disobedience, nor trasgressing due limits, then he is guiltless." (2:173)

The Prophet ﷺ says:

"Whoever forgetfully eats or drinks while fasting should complete his fast; for it is Allâh who has fed him given him to drink." *(Al-Bukhârî* and *Muslim)*

"There is no need for compensation for someone who has been overcome by vomiting while fasting." *(Al-Hâkim)*

"My followers [i.e. Muslims] are excused for [unintentional] error, forgetfulness and that which they have been forced to do against their will." *(At-Tabarânî)*

A Simple and Easy Religion

A Complete Way of Life

Islam is an all-embracing way of life. It extends over the entire spectrum of life showing how to conduct all human activities in a sound and wholesome manner. It does not allow a hierarchy of priests or intermediaries between God and human beings, no far-fetched abstractions, and no complicated rites and rituals. Everybody can readily understand the Qur'ân and follow in the footsteps of the Prophet ﷺ, to the best of his or her ability, assured by Allâh that He will accept from each soul just such duty as it has the ability to offer:

> "On no soul does Allâh place a burden greater than it can bear." (2:286)

When we read the Qur'ân or the Prophetic traditions, we find instructions in all aspects of life, political, social, economic, material, ethical, national and international. These instructions provide us with all the details needed to perform a certain act. The Prophetic traditions go as far as showing us all the steps we need to follow even how to use the toilet: supplications upon entering it and leaving it, which hand to use in order to clean ourselves, and so on. In a word, Islam governs a Muslim's life in all its aspects. This is the reason why it is not only a religion but also a way of life.

Islam does not recognize any kind of separation between religion and life. It openly rejects the western saying, "Render unto Caesar what is Caesar's, and unto God what is God's"; for every thing should be dedicated to God alone; and a Muslim is required to submit himself completely to the Will of Allâh in all his affairs:

> "Say: 'Truly, my prayer, my sacrifice, my living and my dying are for Allâh, the Lord of the worlds. No partner has He: this am I commanded, and I am the first of those who submit to His Will." (6:162)

Islam does not believe in wishful thinking. It clearly states that righteous conduct must be followed by belief in Allâh. The Qur'ân says:

> "For those who believe and work deeds of righteousness is a reward that will never [fail]." (41:8)

> "Those who believe and work righteousness, joy is for them and a blissful place of [final] return." (13:29)

A Complete Way of Life

A Mercy for All the Nation

Islam is a universal religion. The Messengers prior to the advent of the Prophet Muhammad ﷺ were sent to their respective peoples, as the Qur'ân says:

> "We did indeed send, before you, Messengers to their [respective] peoples, and they came to them with clear signs." (30:47)

The Prophet Muhammad ﷺ was not sent to a particular tribe race or set of people, but rather to all mankind, as the Qur'ân says:

> "We have not sent you but as a Messenger to all mankind, giving them glad tidings, and warning them [against sin], but most of men know not." (34:28)

> "Say: 'O mankind! I am sent unto you all, as the Messenger of Allâh, to Whom belongs the dominion of the heavens and the earth'." (7:158)

> "We sent you not but as a mercy for all the nations." (21:107)

These and similar other Verses of the Qur'ân point to the fact that there is now no question of race or nation, of a "chosen people" or the "seed of Abraham" or that of David; of Jew or Gentile, Arab or non-Arab, white or colored. The expression

"all mankind" in the above-mentioned Verses point to the universal and everlasting character of the message of Islam.

It is worthwhile to note here that all the Messengers before Muhammad ﷺ came with certain miracles to lend support to the message with which Allâh had sent them. These miracles were confined to their time and the place where they were sent. Moses had a rod which, when he threw it, would turn into a snake. He did this in the presence of the Pharaoh to prove to him and to his magicians that he was truly sent from God. This snake quickly swallowed up the magicians' ropes and rods that seemed to move about like snakes. He also used it to strike a dry path for his followers through the Red Sea into the Sinai Peninsula. They crossed on foot while Pharaoh, who came in pursuit with his troops, was overwhelmed by the sea. He and his men all perished while Moses and his followers safely crossed the sea.

Jesus Christ, son of Mary, who had a miraculous birth, was also supported with certain miracles, which were restricted to his time. He would, by Allâh's leave, make out of clay the figure of a bird and breathe into it, then it became a real bird with flesh and blood! He would also cure the blind and the lepers, raise the dead and inform the people of what they ate and stored in their homes, by Allâh's leave!

The Prophet Muhammad ﷺ was also supported with numerous miracles, the greatest of all is the Noble Qur'ân which is still in its original form and which will continue to guide people and illuminate their hearts and souls till the Day of Judgment! The Qur'ân is Allâh's Word and whoever earnestly wishes true guidance should read and study the Qur'ân:

A Mercy for All the Nation

"If there were a Qur'ân with which mountains could be moved [from their places], or the earth could be cloven asunder or the dead could be made to speak [this would be the one!]." (13:31)

The Qur'ân has no dark corners or ambiguous expressions. It speaks clearly and guides to the right path. It is straight, clear and understandable. Therein no confusion is to be found:

Praise be to Allâh Who has sent to His servant [i.e., Muhammad ﷺ] the Book and has allowed therein no crookedness. [He has made it] straight [and clear] in order that He may warn [the disbelievers] of a terrible punishment from Him, and that He may give glad tidings to the believers who work righteous deeds, that they shall have a goodly reward, wherein they shall remain for ever." (18:1-2)

It is a guide to all, and to those who accept its guidance, a source of mercy and the way to salvation. Allâh instructs us to earnestly seek to understand it:

"Do they not then earnestly seek to understand the Qur'ân, or is that there are locks upon their hearts?" (47:24)

It is not meant for one class or race; it is universal and is addressed to all the worlds:

"Verily this is no less than a message to all the worlds." (81:27)

The fact that it is still with us in its original form is a clear indication of the universality of Islam.

A Mercy for All the Nation

Moderation in All Spheres of Life

Islam stresses moderation in everything and commands its followers to eschew all extravagances in any direction. It takes deep interest in the spiritual as well as the material well-being of man. It commands its followers to prepare themselves for the Hereafter while at the same time lawfully enjoying their portion of life as long as they do not transgress the limits set by Allâh. The Qur'ân says:

> "Seek, with [the wealth] which Allâh has bestowed on you, the Home of the Hereafter, nor forget your portion in this world." (28:77)

'Ali ﷺ, son of Abu Tâlib, the fourth rightly-guided caliph, said:

> "Work for your life as though you are going to live forever, and work for your Hereafter as though you are going to die tomorrow."

Once the prayers are performed, the believers are encouraged to go about their business:

> "And when the prayer is finished, then disperse in the land and seek of Allâh's Bounty, and remember Allâh frequently that you may prosper." (26:10)

The Islamic course is one of equitable and realistic moderation and the Qur'ân calls Muslims a just nation:

"Thus have We made of you a just (and the best) nation, justly balanced." (2:143)

Unlike other religions and ideologies, Islam does not stress the spiritual at the expense of the material, or vice versa. Rather, it brings both of them into harmony. Islam commends moderation while observing our religious duties and strongly condemns going to the extremes in this respect. Following the middle course in worship is the best alternative as well as the natural way of discharging our duties towards our Creator. Islam prohibits us from overburdening ourselves with duties that are bound to put us off the religion altogether. It requires us to discharge our duties within our capacity, and to the best of our ability. The Qur'ân says:

"Allâh intends for you ease, and He does not want to make things difficult for you." (2:185)

"On no soul does Allâh place a burden greater than it can bear." (2:286)

'Abdullâh bin Jâbir رضى الله عنهما said: "I used to offer all the prayers behind the Prophet ﷺ, and I noticed that his prayer was of moderate length and his sermon, too, was of moderate length." *(Muslim)*

Al-Bukhârî and *Muslim* report that three people came to the house of the Prophet ﷺ to inquire about his way of worship. When they were informed thereof, they considered their own worship insignificant and said, "We are no way near the way

Moderation in All Spheres of Life

of offering his worship while Allâh has forgiven his past and future sins." One of them said, "I will engage in devotions all night long." Another said, "I will fast every single day and I will never miss a day without fasting." The third one said, "I will keep away from women and I will never get married." When the Prophet ﷺ was informed of what they had said, he called them and said to them, "By Allâh! I fear Allâh more than all of you, and I am the most dutiful of all of you to Him. But I sometimes fast and sometimes I don't; I perform *Salât* [prayer] for a part of the night and sleep, and I marry women. So whoever turns away from my way [of life] is not of me."

Islam commands its followers to take a middle course between being stingy and extravagance, be it in their ordinary spending or in charity. They should strike a perfectly just measure between the two extremes. The Qru'ân says:

> "And let not your hand be tied [like a miser] to your neck, nor stretch it forth to its utmost reach [like a spendthrift's], lest you become blameworthy and destitute." (17:29)

The Qur'ân describes the devoted slaves of Allâh as those who:

> "When they spend, are neither extravagant nor stingy but hold a medium [way] between those [extremes]." (25:67)

The Qur'ân even calls spendthrifts "brothers of Satan" because of their foolishness. The Satan fell by his ingratitude

Moderation in All Spheres of Life

to Allâh, so those who misuse or squander Allâh's gifts are also ungrateful to Allâh:

> "And render to the kindred their due rights and to the poor and to the wayfarer, but squander not [your wealth] in the manner of a spendthrift. Verily spendthrifts are brothers of Satan. And the Satan is ever ungrateful to his Lord." (17:26-7)

Committing excess or waste is strictly forbidden:

> "Waste not by excess, for Allâh loves not the wasters." (6:141)

> "Eat and drink, but waste not, for Allâh loves not the wasters." (7:31)

The Prophet ﷺ says:

> "The children of Adam have not filled a 'vessel' worse than their stomachs. A few morsels would be sufficiet for them to keep soul and body together. If they have to, then they should allow a third for their food, a third for their drink and a third for easy breathing." *(Al-Tirmidhî and Ibn Mâjah).*

The Qur'ân condemns the Jews and the Christians because of the excesses they had committed in their religion:

> "O People of the Book! Do not exceed the limits set in your religion, nor say of Allâh anything but the truth. Jesus Christ, the son of Mary, was [no more than] a Messenger of Allâh and His Word, which He

Moderation in All Spheres of Life

bestowed on Mary and a spirit created by Him; so believe in Allâh and His Messengers. Say not 'Three [Trinity]'! Cease! It is better for you. For Allâh is One God, glory be to Him. Far Exalted is He above having a son. To Him belong all that is in the heavens and in the earth. And sufficient is Allâh as a Disposer of affairs." (4:171)

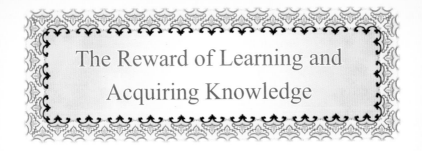

The Reward of Learning and Acquiring Knowledge

Islam brought Knowledge when the whole world was engulfed in utter ignorance. The first Verse the Prophet of Islam received from Allâh was:

"Read! In the Name of your Lord Who has created [all that exists]. He has created man from a clot [a piece of thick coagulated blood]. Read! And your Lord is the Most Bountiful, Who has taught [writing] by the pen. He has taught man that which he knew not." (96:1-5)

This Verse represents the first spark ever to dispel the darkness of ignorance in which the world had been immersed. It awakened in man the faculty of thinking and urged him to worship the true God. It is through knowledge that we can understand Allâh better and serve him better. The Prophet ﷺ states in a tradition that Allâh does not like to be worshipped out of ignorance. The early generation of Muslims became in a matter of a few years a nation knowledgeable in religious as well as in worldly matters, after having groped in the darkness of ignorance for centuries. Allâh reminds the Muslims of His immeasurable bounties :

"He raised among the unlettered people a Messenger from among themselves, reciting unto them His Verses purifying them and teaching them the Book and

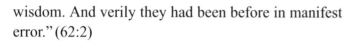

wisdom. And verily they had been before in manifest error." (62:2)

Knowledge is of two types: religious, which has to do with the understanding of the religious duties one is required to carry out, and temporal, which has to do with the matters of this world. A Muslim is required to acquire both types of knowledge. Religious knowledge is a must because without it one will not be able to discharge the enjoined duties in the prescribed manner. The Prophet ﷺ says:

> "Allâh will grant the knowledge of Islam to whoever He wants good for him." *(Al-Bukhârî* and *Muslim)*

Islam encourages the acquisition of knowledge and makes clear its great reward. The Prophet ﷺ says:

> "Allâh makes the way to Paradise easy for him who treads the Path in search of knowledge." (*Muslim*)

> "He who goes forth in search of knowledge will be in Allâh's way until he returns." *(At-Tirmidhî)*

> "He who follows a path in quest of knowledge, Allâh will make the path to Paradise easy for him. The angels lower their wings for the seeker of knowledge, being pleased with what he does. The inhabitants of the heavens and the earth and even the fish in the depth of the oceans seek forgiveness for him. The superiority of the learned person over the devout worshipper is like that of the moon over the rest of the stars. The learned are the heirs of the Prophets; the Prophets bequeath neither dinar nor dirham but only knowledge; and he who acquires it has in fact acquired an abundant portion." (*At-Tirmidhî*)

Beneficial temporal knowledge is also a must and Muslims are encouraged to acquire it in order to benefit themselves and their fellowmen. When the early Muslims understood this fact, they excelled all other nations and carried the torch of knowledge for many centuries. As T.W. Wallbank and A. Schrier put it:

"In medicine, mathematics, astronomy, chemistry and physics, Muslims' achievements were particularly noteworthy. Well-equipped hospitals, usually associated with medical schools, were located in the principal cities. At a time when superstition still hampered the practice of medicine in western countries, Muslim physicians were diagnosing diseases, prescribing cures and performing advanced surgery...Probably the greatest of all physicians was the 9th century figure Al-Razi, known in the West as Rhazes. He was the author of scores of scientific works, including a comprehensive medical encyclopaedia and a pioneering handbook on smallpox and measles. A 10th century physician, Avicenna, compiled a huge *Cannon of Medicine* which was considered the standard guide in european medical circles until the late 17th century... Important advances were made in algebra, analytical geometry and plane spherical trigonometry."[1]

In Islam anything that is considered to be beneficial in one's spiritual or worldly advancement is encouraged and advocated. After all, the acquisition of knowledge is, as the Prophet of Islam makes it clear, "an obligation upon every Muslim man and woman." (*Ibn Mâjah*)

Allâh commands the Prophet ﷺ to invoke Him to advance him in knowledge:

> "Say: 'O my Lord! Increase me in knowledge.'" (20:114)

It is a fact that Faith makes all people equal before Allâh, but there is leadership and rank and degree, joined with greater or lesser responsibility, and that depends on true knowledge and insight, namely the knowledge of religion:

> "Allâh will exalt in degree those of you who believe and those who have been granted knowledge." (58:11)

1 *Living World History,* Scott Forseman and Company, 1990,pp. 191-2.

The Reward of Learning and Acquiring Knowledge

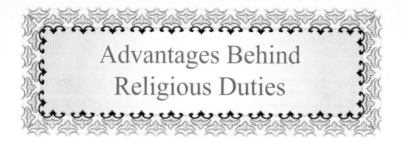

Fair-minded researchers and objective observers acknowledge the fact that all Divine commands are beneficial to mankind and that all Divine prohibitions are harmful in one way or another. A closer look at the rulings of Islam will reveal to the discerning person the greatness and nobility of this religion. Islam calls to nobility, truthfulness, chastity, justice, fulfilling the covenant, safeguarding trusts, displaying kindness to orphans and the poor, maintaining neighborliness, honoring the guest and enjoying the lawful worldly pleasures in moderation. It calls to righteouness and piety, and forbids sin and transgression. In a word, it calls to all that brings about happiness and forbids all that is bound to trigger loss and ruin.

Islam provides a better alternative for each and every thing it has declared forbidden and unlawful. Divination by arrows [for ascertaining lucky or unlucky moments or whether one should undertake certain actions or not] has been superseded by another form of *Salât* [prayer], namely *Salâtul-Istikhârah*. In this prayer one sincerely prays to Allâh, the Omniscient and Wise, to guide him to what is beneficial and keep him away from what may be harmful. Usurious transactions have been superseded by lawful, profitable trade; alcoholic beverages have been superseded by

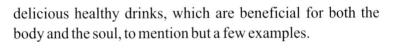

delicious healthy drinks, which are beneficial for both the body and the soul, to mention but a few examples.

If we trace all the Islamic teachings, we will certainly find that Allâh, Who knows what is best for us, has not prohibited us something without providing us with a better alternative of the same nature. We shall briefly consider below some of the advantages and beauty of *Salât* [prayer], *Zakât* [obligatory charity], fasting, *Hajj* [pilgrimage] and *Jihâd* [fighting or struggling in Allâh's way].

Salât [prayer] - a Unique Spiritual Experience

Salât [prayer] is a great act of worship, which brings those who observe it closer to their Creator. It is a unique spiritual experience where every muscle of the body joins the soul and the mind in the worship and glorification of Allâh. It inculcates sincerity and total devotion in the hearts of those who perform it. It makes them stand before Allâh in humility, exalting Him and invoking Him. They begin it by saying *"Allâhu Akbar"*, acknowledging that Allâh is the Greatest, Who Alone is to be exalted and worshipped. They then engage in praising Him in a manner suiting His Majesty. They devote themselves completely to Him and totally submit to His Will, seeking His help to keep them on the straight path, that of the devout and the pious, and to guard them against the path of those who have gone astray

and have thus earned His wrath. When they reach the climax of worship during *Salât,* and their hearts are deeply imbued with awe and reverence, they prostrate before Him, placing the most honored part of the body on the floor, showing great submission and humility.

The excellence of *Salât* [prayer] is matchless and its virtues are boundless. Those who observe it in the prescribed manner acknowledge the Greatness of Allâh and their hearts experience a singular feeling of awe and fear of Him that helps them in shunning all sinful acts by providing them a chance of direct communion with their Creator five times a day. It is no wonder then that the Qur'ân says:

"Observe *Salât* [prayer]. Surely, *Salât* restrains [one] from indecency and manifest evil; and remembrance of Allâh indeed is the greatest virtue." (29:45)

It teaches them to observe punctuality as it is prescribed at stated times:

"Verily, *Salât* is enjoined on the believers at fixed hours." (4:103)

It is also an abundant source of courage and patience and a great aid in times of distress and difficulty. The Qur'ân says:

"And seek help in patience and *Salât.*" (2:45)

When they observe it regularly, they develop a strong desire to do righteous deeds, anticipating Allâh's reward in the Hereafter. When they perform it in congregation, they establish strong social relationships with others and they strengthen these brotherly ties with such qualities as love, tenderness, respect and co-operation.

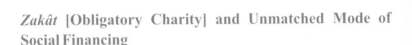

Zakât [Obligatory Charity] and Unmatched Mode of Social Financing

Next to *Salât* [prayer], *Zakât* is the most important of the religious duties enjoined on the Muslims. It assumes a religious sanctity, which is unmatched by any mode of social finance anywhere else. There is no ready equivalent word in the English language for this exceptionally remarkable institution. It does not only signify a form of charity, as many people think. The word is comprehensive and includes a number of meanings. As Hamudah Abdul-'Âti simply puts it:

"It is not just a form of charity or almsgiving or tax or tithe. Nor is it simply an expression of kindness; it is all of these combined and much more. It is not merely a deduction of a certain percentage from one's property, but an abundant enrichment and spiritual investment. It is not simply a voluntary contribution to someone or some cause, nor is it a government tax that a shrewd clever person can get away with. Rather, it is a duty enjoined by Allâh and undertaken by Muslims in the interest of society as a whole... It combines with all these [meanings] God-mindedness and spiritual as well as moral motives. That is why there can be no equivalent to the word *Zakât* because of the supreme originality of the Qur'ân, the Divine Book of Allâh." [1]

Zakât has myriad advantages and far-reaching effects in the Muslim society. It is a clear expression of affection towards the poor and the needy, which helps satisfy their needs and

---

1. Hammudah Abdalati, *Islam in Focus,* American Trust Publicaton, p.95.

settle their debts. The literal meaning of *Zakât* in Arabic is purification: It purifies not only the benefactor's heart from selfishness and thirst for wealth but his property as well; for Allâh will certainly bless it and make it increase. It also purifies the heart of the recipient from envy, jealousy and hatred, and fosters in his heart goodwill towards the contributor. It instills in the believers generosity, and purifies their heart from being self-centered and greedy for wealth. It is a panacea to many social evils and a sure cure for being stingy. The Qur'ân says:

"And whoever is saved from his own covetousness, such are they who will be successful." (59:9)

When *Zakât* is paid in the prescribed manner, it renders corrupt systems like communism and capitalism as unnecessary, letting peace and progress prevail.

The object of *Zakât* is to provide relief for the distressed and promotion of the welfare of the economically less favored sections of the community. It also discourages the hoarding of money and commodities, and thus ensures a brisk circulation of both, resulting in a healthy economy.

The Qur'ân expressly enjoins that wealth should not be permitted to accumulate in a few hands and that it ought to be kept constantly in circulation in order that:

"...It may not become a fortune used by the rich among you." (59:7)

To achieve this, it prohibits the lending of money on interest by means of which a few clever people are able to monopolize the greater part of the wealth of the community, and makes provision for the compulsory distribution of inheritance. It does not permit any person to leave the whole of their property to one out of several heirs to augment the share of one heir at the expense of another. It seeks to bring about equitable adjustment in the distribution of wealth through the *Zakât*. It imposes as a first charge upon all government revenues and resources the obligation of providing for the welfare and progress of the poorer sections of the community. Through these means, it provides for the economic prosperity of all sections of the people.

Saum [Fasting] helps develop a Strong Personality and Character

Fasting or *Saum* is a unique moral and spiritual Islamic attribute. Its beauties and merits are limitless. The main reason behind fasting is to attain the noble status of *Taqwa*, or piety or righteousness, as the Qur'ân says:

> "O you who believe! Fasting is prescribed to you as it was prescribed to those before you, that you may become pious." (2:183)

Fasting helps the faithful develop a strong personality and character. It instills in them the noble quality of will power and determination. For when one fasts, one certainly learns to discipline one's passionate desires and places oneself in opposition to physical temptations.

It also helps them develop the virtue of displaying affection towards the poor and the distressed; when one observes fasting and undergoes the pangs of hunger, one actually remembers the condition and distress of the poor. It also reminds them of Allâh's favor upon them when they experience hunger while fasting; this reminder prompts them to give thanks to Him for His endless bounties.

Fasting also develops the valuable quality of patience and nurtures a gentle and forbearing character. Fasting in Islam is equal in reward to half the reward of patience, and patience in its turn is equal to half the reward of Faith. The Prophet ﷺ says:

"Ramadân is the month of patience and endurance."

Fasting is also a shield against many diseases. It provides one with both spiritual growth and physical fitness. It strengthens the body and is a cure to many known diseases. It helps relax one's digestive system and cause the body to get rid of accumulated pollutants which are detrimental to health.

Besides all the above benefits it is also an act of worship that testifies to total submission and obedience to Allâh. The hardship one endures while carrying out this obligation is insignificant in comparison with the noble objective one seeks to attain, namely Allâh's Pleasure and the great reward in the Hereafter.

A part of the obligation attached to the Islamic fast is that, apart from abstention from food, drink and sexual intercourse during the hours of fasting, a Muslim must make special efforts to attain higher standards of virtue and purity. One lesson that fasting teaches us is that a person who abstains from the use of permissible things during the fast should on no account indulge in that which is prohibited.

Indeed, the month of Ramadân is analogous to an educational institution, which nurtures virtue and piety. For when a Muslim fasts he not only abstains from food, drink and lawful sexual intercourse but also tries hard, to the best of his ability, to shun all evil actions that are bound to invalidate his fast. The Prophet ﷺ says:

> "If one of you is fasting, he should not use obscene language or behave foolishly and impudently; and if someone fights with him or abuses him, he should say: 'I am fasting! I am fasting!'" *(Al-Bukhârî and Muslim)*

> "Whoever does not abstain from deceitful speech and actions [while fasting], Allâh is not in need of him leaving his food and drink." *(Al-Bukhârî)*

Hajj [Pilgrimage] an Obligation with innumerable Merits

Hajj is another great obligation, which has innumerable merits. It creates for those who perform it, an occasion to meet and know one another, to exchange views and compare experiences and unite their efforts for the common good.

Hajj purifies the soul and nurtures such noble qualities as generosity, fortitude and modesty. Those who perform it are commanded to avoid all forms of wickedness and observe patience and perseverance. The Qur'ân says:

> "The *Hajj* is [in] the well-known months [by the lunar year]. So whoever intends to perform it therein, let there be no obscenity, nor wickedness, nor wrangling in the *Hajj*." (2:197)

It is a wholesome demonstration of the universality of Islam. It helps bring together myriad races from the four corners of the earth to worship, in all humility, one single God in one special place, during one special season. Distances are annihilated; divergences of race and color are set aside in this fraternity of faith that unites all Muslims in one great brotherhood. Muslims feel they are all on equal footing.

Hajj also provides a good occasion to travel in the land to find out about its people and their customs and traditions and also to discover the land of revelations where many Prophets and Messengers called to the worship of Allâh alone.

Hajj also provides a good occasion to travel in the land to find out about its people and their customs and traditions and

Advantages Behind Religious Duties

also to discover the land of revelations where many Prophets and Messengers called to the worship of Allâh alone.

Hajj also reminds those who perform it of the Day of Resurrection when all human beings will stand equal before the Lord of the worlds for judgment, barefooted, naked and uncircumcised. It also serves the noble purpose of providing for the final journey into the future world, that of the Hereafter. For one cannot provide such provisions except in this very life. The Qur'ân says:

"A n d   f u r n i s h yourselves with [necessary] provisions, and surely, the best provision is righteousness." (2:197)

Hajj also opens our eyes to death and keeps our mind alert to it. For once we assume the state of *Ihram* [a state in which one is prohibited to practice certain deeds that are lawful at other times. *'Umrah* and *Hajj* are performed during such state, two sheets of unstitched clothes are the only clothes one wears], as regards appearance, we actually rid ourselves of the clothes of the living and put on two sheets of unstitched clothes, which remind us of the shrouds in which the dead are wrapped for burial. This mere thought prompts us to strive hard in preparation for the Hereafter.

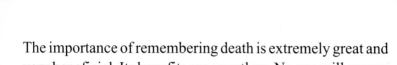

The importance of remembering death is extremely great and very beneficial. Its benefits are countless. No one will escape death and all mankind will eventually stand before Allâh for reckoning. The Qur'ân says:

> "Every soul shall have a taste of death, and only on the Day of Judgment shall you be paid your full recompense. Only he who is saved from the Fire and admitted to the Garden will have succeeded. For the life of this world is but goods and chattels of deception." (3:185)

The Prophet ﷺ describes death in very horrifying terms: "the Destroyer of pleasures". This mere thought stirs one to righteous works with a view to attaining Allâh's Pleasure. Life is but a period of probation after which everyone will see what he has done. Indeed, it is a fleeting, deceptive show that should not be trusted.

Remembering death certainly helps us mend our ways and try our best to work righteous good deeds and ward off evil actions. Were all human beings aware of the manifold benefits of remembering death, justice would certainly be easy to administer and peace and progress would definitely prevail. *Hajj* provides for this opportunity to remember death.

Jihâd [Striving in the way of Allâh] the only way to uproot Injustice

Jihâd [fighting or struggling] in the way of Allâh has

countless advantages. It serves to grant victory to Allâh's religion and to His devout slaves. It serves to raise mankind from the class of animals, which are devoid of the faculty of intellect. The Qur'ân says:

"Many are the jinn and men We have made for Hell: they have hearts wherewith they understand not, and they have eyes wherewith they see not, and they have ears wherewith they hear not. They are like cattle; nay, they are even more astray. They are indeed quite heedless." (7:179)

Jihâd also gives those who participate in it, dignified life in this world and bliss for all eternity. If they are granted victory

over their enemy, they will raise the flag of Truth high; on the other hand, if they are slain in the struggle, they will certainly attain the true real life, to which the transient life in this world is but a shadow. The Qur'ân says:

"Think not of those who are slain in the way of Allâh as

dead. Nay, they are alive, finding sustenance from their Lord." (3:169)

In fact, *Jihâd* testifies to the truthfulness, sincerity and total obedience of those who wage it for the sake of Allâh. It also uproots injustice and gives people the freedom to worship the True God in peace without fear of persecution. The Qur'ân says:

"And fight them on until there is no more persecution and the religion is [freely professed] for Allâh." (2:193)

Forsaking *Jihâd* definitely leads to humiliation:

"If you practice *Bai' Al- 'Înah* [i.e., selling goods to a person for a certain price and then buying them back from him for a far less price], follow the tails of the cows [i.e., be indulged in agriculture and become contented with it], and desert *Jihâd* Allâh will afflict you with humiliation, and He will not relieve you from it until you return to your religion." (*Abu Dâwûd*)

Jihâd also testifies to one's sincerity and safety from hypocrisy, as evidenced by the following *Hadith* in which the Prophet ﷺ says:

"Whoever dies while he has never thought of fighting *Jihâd* in Allâh's way, will die as a hypocrite." (*Abu Dâwûd*)

Perhaps it is appropriate to mention here the fact that Islam

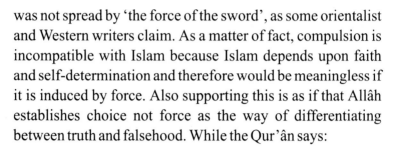

was not spread by 'the force of the sword', as some orientalist and Western writers claim. As a matter of fact, compulsion is incompatible with Islam because Islam depends upon faith and self-determination and therefore would be meaningless if it is induced by force. Also supporting this is as if that Allâh establishes choice not force as the way of differentiating between truth and falsehood. While the Qur'ân says:

"Let there be no compulsion in religion: Truth stands out clear from falsehood." (2:256)

The Beauty as seen by Others

The 'beauty of Islam' has in fact conquered the hearts of millions of people and won them into its fold. They have found its principles straightforward and its all-inclusive teachings practical and beneficial to all mankind. Let us look at some of what these people have said.

German social scientist and diplomat Wilfried Hofman [now Murad Hofman] says:

"For some time now, striving for more and more precision and brevity, I have tried to put on paper, in a systematic way, all philosophical truths, which, in my view, can be ascertained beyond reasonable doubt. In the course of this effort, it dawned on me that the typical attitude of an agnostic is not an intelligent one. Man simply cannot escape a decision to believe. The createdness of what exists around us is obvious; that Islam undoubtedly finds itself in the 'greatest harmony with overall reality. Thus I realize, not without shock, that step by step, in spite of myself and almost unconsciously, in feeling and thinking I have grown into a Muslim. Only one last step remained to be taken: to formalize my conversion. As of today I am a

Muslim. I have arrived."[1]

Speaking to the daily *Al-Madinah,* Jeddah, 15 July 1989, the former world heavyweight champion boxer Cassius Clay [now Muhammad Ali Clay] says:

> "I have had many beautiful moments in my life. But the feelings I had while standing on Mount Arafât on the day of the *Hajj* [Muslim pilgrimage] was the most unique. I felt exalted by the indescribable spiritual atmosphere there as over a million and a half pilgrims invoked Allâh to forgive them of their sins and bestow upon them His choicest blessings. It was an exhilarating experience to see people belonging to different colors, races and nationalities; kings, heads of states and ordinary men from very poor countries, all clad in two simple white sheets praying to Allâh without any sense of either pride or inferiority. It was a practical manifestation of the concept of the equality of Islam."[2]

Austrian Leopold Weiss [now Muhammad Asad] says:

> "Since I became a Muslim I have been asked, time and again: 'Why did you embrace Islam? What was it that attracted you particularly?' And I must confess: I do not know of any satisfactory answer. It was not any particular teaching that attracted me, but the whole

---

1   *The Sword of Islam,* WAMY series on Islam, N13, pp. 4 & 5.

2   ibid., p.6.

wonderful, inexplicably coherent structure of moral teaching and the practical program of life. I could not say, even now, which aspect of it appeals to me more than any other. Islam appears to me like a perfect work of architecture. All its parts are harmoniously conceived to complement and support each other; nothing is superfluous and nothing lacking, with the result of an absolute balance and solid composure. Probably this feeling that everything in the teachings and postulates of Islam is 'in its proper place,' has created the strongest impression on me. There might have been, along with it, other impressions also which today it is difficult for me to analyze. After all, it was a matter of love; and love is composed of many things; of our desires and our loneliness, of our high aims and our shortcomings, of our strength and our weakness. So it was in my case. Islam came over me like a robber who enters a house by night; but, unlike a robber, it entered to remain for good." [1]

German diplomat and social worker Muhammad A. Hobohm says:

"*Why do Westerners embrace Islam*? There are various reasons for it. In the first place, truth always has its force. The basic tenets of Islam are so rational, so natural and so appealing that an honest truth-seeker cannot help being impressed by them. To take, for

---

1   *Islam – Our Choice,* the abridged edition, 1992, compiled & edited by Ebrahim F. Bawany, pp. 21 & 22.

example, the belief in monotheism: How it raises the dignity of man and how it frees us from the grip of superstition! How naturally it leads to the equality of men, for all have been created by the same God and all are servants of the same Lord. For the Germans, in particular, the belief in God is a source of inspiration, source of fearless courage and a source of the feeling of security. Then the idea of life after death turns the tables. Life in this world is no longer the main objective, and a great part of our human energy is devoted to the betterment of our Hereafter. Faith in the Day of Judgement automatically spurs a man to give up misdeeds, for good deeds alone can ensure eternal salvation, although wrong deeds may prosper here for a limited period. The belief that none can escape the consequences of the judgment of a Just, Impartial and Omniscient Lord makes one think twice before one does anything wrong and surely this internal check is more effective than the most efficient police force in the world.

Another thing that attracts foreigners to Islam is its emphasis on tolerance. Then the daily prayers teach one punctuality and the one-month fasting enables one to exercise self-control, and without doubt punctuality and self-discipline are two of the most important attributes of a good man and a great man.

Now comes the real achievement of Islam. It is the only

The Beauty as seen by Others

ideology, which has succeeded in instilling in its followers the spirit of observing ethical and moral limitations without external compulsion. A Muslim knows that, wherever he is, he is being observed by God. This belief keeps him away from sin. As man is naturally inclined towards goodness, Islam also offers peace of mind and heart–and this is what is totally absent from the Western society of today.

I have lived under different systems of life and have had the opportunity of studying various ideologies, but have come to the conclusion that none is as perfect as Islam.

Communism has its attractions, so has secular democracy and Nazism. But none has got a complete code of a noble life. Only Islam has it, and that is why good men embrace it.

Islam is not theoretical; it is practical. Islam is not departmental affair; it means complete submission to the will of God." [1]

Devis Warrington Fry from Australia says:

"Islam came to me as the spring comes to the cold earth after dark winter. It has warmed my soul and clothed me in beautiful teachings. How logical! 'There is but one God and Muhammad is His Prophet.' Can there be anything more sublime than

The Beauty as seen by Others

---

1   ibid., pp. 30-31

this? None of the mysterious 'the Father, the Son and the Holy Ghost' ritual, which I suppose, is quite awe-inspiring but is hardly satisfactory to a keen mind. Islam is so modern, so applicable to the world today." [1]

T. H Mcbarklise from Ireland writes:

"The broad outlook of Islam compared to the narrow view of the Christian sects, the learning and culture of Islamic countries in the Middle Ages compared with the ignorance and superstition of other lands at that time, the logical theory of compensation as opposed to the Christian idea of atonement, were a few of the points that first struck me. Later I came to realize that here was a faith broad as humanity itself, ready for the guidance of rich and poor alike and able to break down all barriers of creed and color." [2]

American poet, critic and author Colonel Donald S. Rockwell writes:

"The simplicity of Islam, the powerful appeal and the compelling atmosphere of its mosques, the earnestness of its faithful followers, the confidence inspiring realization of millions throughout the world who answer the five daily calls to prayer, these factors attracted me from the first. But after I had determined to become a follower of Islam, I found many deeper reasons for confirming my decision. The mellow

---

1   ibid., p. 106

2   ibid., p. 105

concept of life-fruit of the Prophet's combined course of action and contemplation, the wise counsel, the admonitions to charity and mercy. The broad humanitarianism, the pioneer declaration of women's rights, these and other factors of the teachings of the man of Makkah were to me among the first obvious evidence of a practical religion so tersely and so aptly epitomized in the cryptic words of Muhammad, 'Trust in God and tie your camel.' He gave us a religious system of normal action, not blind faith in the protection of an unseen force in spite of our own neglect, but confidence that if we do all things rightly and to the best of our ability, we may trust in what comes as the Will of God... When I stood in the inspiring mosques of Istanbul, Damascus, Jerusalem, Cairo, Algiers, Tangier, Fez and other cities, I was conscious of a powerful reaction the potent uplift of Islam's simple appeal to the sense of higher things, unaided by elaborate trappings, ornamentation, figures, pictures, music and ceremonial ritual. The mosque is a place of quiet contemplation and self-effacement in the greater reality of the God. The democracy of Islam has always appealed to me. Potentate and pauper have the same rights on the floor of the mosque, on their knees in humble worship. There are no rented pews or special reserved seats.

The Muslim accepts no man as mediator between himself and his God. He goes direct to the invisible source of creation and life, God, without reliance on a

The Beauty as seen by Others

saving formula of repentance of sins and belief in the power of a teacher to afford him salvation. The universal brotherhood of Islam, regardless of race, politics, color or country, has been brought home to me most keenly many times in my life, and this is another feature which drew me towards the Faith." [1]

The baseless claim that Islam converted the peoples it had 'conquered by force' has also been refuted by prominent non-Muslims. Mahatma Gandhi, for instance, writes in *Young Indian,* 1924:

"I became more than ever convinced that it was not the sword that won a place for Islam in those days in the scheme of life. It was the rigid simplicity, the utter self-effacement of the Prophet, the scrupulous regard for his pledges, his intense devotion to his friends and followers, his intrepidity, his absolute trust in God and his own mission. These, and not the sword carried everything before them and surmounted every trouble." [2]

S. Tritton writes:

"The picture of the Muslim soldier advancing with a sword in one hand and the Qur'ân in the other is quite false." [3]

James A. Michener writes in the *Reader's Digest*, under the

---

1   ibid., pp. 49-50

2   Quoted in *The Sword of Islam,* p. 6.

3   ibid., p.7

The Beauty as seen by Others

title "Islam–the Misunderstood Religion":

> "No other religion in history spread so rapidly as Islam. The West has widely believed that this surge of religion was made possible by the sword. But no modern scholar accepts that idea, and the Qur'ân is explicit in support of the freedom of conscience." [1]

Laurence E. Browne writes in *The Prospects of Islam*:

> "Incidentally these well-established facts dispose of the idea so widely fostered in Christian writings about the Muslims that wherever they went, forced people to accept Islam at the point of the sword." [2]

De Lay O' Leany also writes in *Islam at Crossroads*, London, 1923, p. 8:

> "History makes it clear, however, that the legend of fanatical Muslims, sweeping through the world and forcing Islam at the point of the sword upon conquered races is one of the most fanatically absurd myths that historians have ever repeated." [3]

It is worthwhile mentioning here that it is absolutely wrong to judge Islam by the deteriorating condition of Muslim and the blatant corruption that pervades the Muslim world. What Islam preaches is one thing and what so many Muslims nowadays practice is something else. The only way whereby we do justice to Islam is to find out about its noble teachings

---

1   ibid., p.6

2   ibid., p.6

3   ibid., p.6

which are clearly set out at length in the Qur'ân and the Prophetic traditions. The famous popular singer Cat Stevens who later embraced Islam once observed:

> "It will be wrong to judge Islam in the light of the behavior of some bad Muslims who are always shown on the media. It is like judging a car as a bad one if the driver is drunk and he bangs it with the wall. Islam guides all human beings in daily life – in its spiritual, mental and physical dimensions. Nevertheless, we must find the sources of these instructions: The Qur'ân and the example of the Prophet. Then we can see the idea of Islam." [1]

What is generally said about Islam in the media and in many academic circles also give a wrong idea about it. As Maurice Bucaille put it:

> "The totally erroneous statements made about Islam in the West are sometimes the result of ignorance, and sometimes of systematic denigration. The most serious of all the untruths told about it are however those dealing with facts for while mistaken opinions are excusable, the presentation of facts running contrary to reality is not. It is disturbing to read blatant untruths in eminently respectable works written by authors who *a priori* are highly qualified." [2]

---

1 ibid., p.4

2 Maurice Bucaille, *The Bible, The Qur'ân & Science*, American Trust Publications, 1979, pp. 110-1.

The Good and the Bad

The commands and prohibitions in Islam are by Allâh Himself for the spiritual and mental well-being as well as the moral and material benefit of all mankind. When the moral principles are stated in Islam as lawful or unlawful, they are designed to build in the human being a sound mind, a peaceful soul, a strong personality and a healthy body. There is no doubt that these are necessary requirements for the general welfare and prosperity of mankind. Allâh is the Creator and knows what is best for his creatures. Talking about some of the characteristics of the unlettered Prophet ﷺ whom the Jews and the Christians find mentioned in their Scriptures, the Torah and the Gospel, the Qur'ân says:

> "He [i.e., Prophet Muhammad ﷺ] commands them what is just and forbids them what is evil. He allows them as lawful what is good [and pure] and prohibits them what is bad [and impure]." (7:157)

This Verse makes it clear that in Islam whatever leads to the well-being of the individual or society, is morally good, and therefore lawful; and whatever is injurious either to society or the individual, is morally bad, and therefore unlawful. Examples of the beauty of Islàm are countless and it is therefore next to impossible to be exhaustive and cite them all. However, we will attempt here to touch on some of the commands and prohibitions in Islam with a view to presenting the reader with a small idea of this beauty. We will draw heavily upon the Qur'ân and the Prophetic Traditions as these are the chief sources of Islam known as the *Sharî`ah* [Islamic jurisprudence].

Commands for the Good

Equality as a Birthright

Islam has given man equality as a birthright and has thus struck at the very root of all artificial barriers of color, race, language, nationality and social status:

> "O mankind! We created you from a single [pair] of a male and female, and made you into nations and tribes, that you may know each other. Verily, the most honorable of you with Allâh is [he who is] the most righteous of you." (49:13)

This Verse is in fact addressed to the entire human race and not only to the Muslim brotherhood, though it is understood that in a perfect world the two would be analogous. As it is, mankind is descended from one pair of parents, namely Adam and Eve. Their tribes, races and nationalities are convenient labels by which we may know certain differing characteristics. These differences do not affect the true stature of man before Allâh. Fallacious concepts of chosen and gentile peoples, social castes and second-rate citizens are obsolete and have no room in Islam. With Allâh, honor belongs to the pious and the upright.

The Prophet ﷺ says:

> "O mankind, your Lord is One and your father is one. You all descend from Adam, and Adam was created from earth. He is most honored among you before Allâh who is most upright. No Arab has any superiority over a non-Arab, nor does a colored person have any superiority over a white person, ora white person any superiority over a colored person except by piety." (*Ahmad* and *At-Tirmidhî*)

Justice under all Circumstances

Islam commands justice and forbids inequity under all circumstances. The Qur'ân says:

> "O you who believe! Be strict in observing justice, and be witnesses for Allâh even though it may be against yourselves or against parents and kindred." (4:135)

> "O you who believe! Be steadfast in the Cause of Allâh, bearing witness in equity and let not a people's enmity incite you to act otherwise than with justice. Be always just, that is nearer to righteousness." (5:8)

Islamic justice is something higher than that prevalent in other societies. It searches out the innermost motives, because we are to act knowing we are in the presence of Allâh Who is Well-Aware of all motives. Islam commands Muslims to administer justice in all aspects of life without fear of anything, even if this seems to be detrimental to their own interests or the interests of those who are near and dear to

Commands for the Good

them:

> "O you who believe! Stand out firmly for justice, as witnesses to Allâh, even though it be against yourselves, or your parents, or your kin, be he rich or poor, for Allâh is a better Protector to both [than you]. So follow not the lusts of your hearts, lest you avoid justice." (4:135)

Justice is to be administered even if it is against rulers, for they are not above the law. A woman belonging to a noble family was arrested in connection with a theft. The case was brought to the Prophet ﷺ and it was recommended that she be spared punishment. The Prophet ﷺ replied:

> "The nations that lived before you were destroyed by Allâh because they punished the common man for their offences and let their dignitaries go unpunished for their crimes. I swear by Him in Whose Hand my soul is, that even if Fâtimah, the daughter of Muhammad had committed this crime, I would have amputated her hand."

During the caliphate of 'Umar ﷺ, Muhammad the son of 'Amr bin Al-'Âs, then governor of Egypt, whipped an Egyptian. The Egyptian went to Al-Madinah and lodged his complaint with the caliph who immediately summoned the governor and his son. When they appeared before him, the caliph handed a whip to the Egyptian plaintiff and asked him to whip the son of the governor is his presence. After the Egyptian had taken his revenge, 'Umar ﷺ said to him "Give

Commands for the Good

one stroke of the whip to the honorable governor as well. His son would certainly not have beaten you were it not for the false pride that he had in his father's high office." The plaintiff submitted: "The person who had beaten me, I have already avenged myself on him." 'Umar ◈ said: "By Allâh, if you had beaten him [the governor] I would not have checked you from doing so. You have spared him of your own free will." Then 'Umar ◈ turned to 'Amr bin Al-'Âs and said angrily: "O 'Amr, when did you start to enslave the people, though they were born free by their mothers?"

Islam forbids injustice in all its forms. It makes it clear that all those who wrong other people and usurp their rights will lose their rewards on the Day of Judgment to the wronged. For Allâh, the Just, does not wrong any one and will establish justice in full on the Day of Judgment. The Prophet ◈ once asked his Companions: "Do you know who is really bankrupt?" They replied: "The bankrupt amongst us is one who has no goods or chattels." To this he said:

> "The [really] bankrupt among my followers is one who will come on the Day of Judgment with a record of *Salât* [prayers], fasting and *Zakât* [obligatory payment against one's wealth]. Because of having abused so-and-so, slandered so-and-so, stolen the property of so-and-so, killed so-and-so, and unlawfully beaten so-and-so, he will have his rewards given to all these [wronged] people; if, however, his rewards are not enough, he will have their sins thrown upon him instead, then he will be thrown in the Fire." *(Muslim)*

Safeguarding the Honor

Islam commands its followers to be self-supporting and to stay away from being a liability on any body. Islam respects all kinds of work for earning one's livelihood so long as there is no indecency or wrong involved. It makes it an obligation for its followers to engage in productive work conscientiously and eschew laziness and begging. According to Islam, the status of honest working men cannot be lowered on account of the work they are doing for a living. In fact, it aims at safeguarding man's honor and self-esteem. The Prophet ﷺ says:

> "It is far better for you to take your ropes, go to the mountain [cut some firewood], carry it on your back, sell it and thereby save your face [against humiliation] than begging from people, whether they give you or not." (*Al-Bukhârî*)

> "Never has anyone eaten a better food then that he has eaten [as a result of work] from his own hand."(*Al-Bukhârî*)

Islam also invites Muslims to observe efficiency while undertaking any work. It teaches them that if a thing is worth doing it is worth doing well. It states that if any of us undertakes any work, God loves to see us do it well and with efficiency.

Commands for the Good

Conduct of Affairs by Mutual Consultation

Islam urges its followers to conduct their affairs by mutual consultation and welcome other people's opinion as long as it is wholly in keeping with correct reasoning and emerges from profound experience. The Qur'ân says:

> "Those [i.e., the pious] who respond to their Lord, establish regular *Salât*, and whose affairs are [decided] by mutual consultation." (42:38)

> "Ask forgiveness for them, and consult them in affairs." (3:159)

Truth at every Cost

Islam also urges its followers to recognize and understand the Creator of the universe and further shape their life firmly and steadfastly according to that Truth and Reality. It teaches them, after attaining this stage of understanding, to remain steadfast and never get tempted by the various crooked currents, ideologies and philosophies to change their course. Steadfastness to one's lofty principles pays off and those who observe it will certainly receive Allâh's reward in this life and in the Hereafter. The Qur'ân says:

> "In the case of those who say, 'Our Lord is Allâh', and further, stand straight and steadfast, the angels descend upon them [at the time of their death, saying:] 'Fear not, nor grieve! But receive the glad tidings of the Garden of Bliss, which you have been promised. We are your friends and protectors in this life and in the

Hereafter: therein shall you have all that you desire; therein shall you have all that you ask for.'" (41:30-31)

Allâh also addresses His Messenger ﷺ thus:

"Therefore stand firm [on the straight path] as you have been commanded, and also those who have turned to Allâh with you." (11:112)

The Prophet's sincere advice to his Companion Sufyân, son of 'Abdullâh, also makes this idea clear:

"Say: 'I believe in Allâh', then remain steadfast."

The Qur'ân says:

"O you who believe! Fear Allâh and be with those who are truthful." (9:119)

The Prophet ﷺ says:

"Give up what seems to you to be doubtful and adhere to that which is not doubtful." (*At-Tirmidhî*)

Kindness to All

In his relationship with his fellow men, a Muslim has a number of obligations to discharge. He must display kindness to his relatives, concern for his neighbor, affection and support for the poor and the orphans, mercy towards the infirm and servants, compassion for the young, respect for the elderly, sympathy for the grieved and cheer for the depressed. The Qur'ân says:

"Worship Allâh and join none with Him in worship, and show kindness to parents, kinsfold, orphans, the poor, the neighbor who is near of kin, the neighbor who is a stranger, the companion by your side, the wayfarer, and those slaves whom your right hand possess."(4:36)

"And lower your wing [of mercy] to the believers who follow you." (26:215)

"Treat not the orphan with oppression, repulse not those who ask [you of anything], and proclaim the Grace of your Lord." (93:9-11)

"Have you seen him who denies the Judgment [to come]? Then such is the one who repulses the orphan and encourages not the feeding of the poor." (107:1-3)

"And what will make you know the path that is steep? It is the freeing of a slave, or feeding in a day of hunger, an orphan near of kin, or an indigent [down] in the dust." (90:12-16)

"He [i.e., the Prophet ﷺ] frowned and turned away, because there came to him the blind man. But what could tell you that but perchance he might be seeking to purify himself, or he may receive admonition, and the reminder might profit him?" (80:1-4)

The incident to which the last Verses refer is that of the Prophet Muhammad ﷺ with a blind man called 'Abdullâh bin Umm Maktûm. The Prophet ﷺ was once deeply and

Commands for the Good

earnestly engaged in attempting to invite the pagan Quraish leaders to Islam when he was interrupted by a blind man who came to learn the Qur'ân and seek satisfaction for his spiritual craving. The Prophet ﷺ naturally disliked the interruption and so he frowned and turned away from him because he was trying to make these leaders' hearts incline towards the Truth and thus get support for Islam. No sooner had the Prophet ﷺ finished talking to the Quraish leaders and was about to return home than he received Revelation which he published without the least hesitation. The Prophet ﷺ always afterwards held the man in high honor and esteem.

This incident reflects the highest honor of the Prophet's sincerity in the Revelation that was vouchsafed to him. The *Surah*, which contains this Verse, provides substantive proof that the Prophet ﷺ was not the author of the Qur'ân, nor the founder of Islam, as some Westerns and orientalists mistakenly claim. Had that been the case, he would not have mentioned this incident as a result of which he received mild reproof from Allâh.

The Prophet ﷺ also says:

> "He who believes in Allâh and the Last Day must not harm his neighbor; he who believes in Allâh and the last day should honor his guest; he who believes in Allâh and the last day should speak good or remain silent." (*Al-Bukhârî* and *Muslim*)

> "By Allâh! He will not be a [true] believer." He

Commands for the Good

repeated this statement three times. His Companions asked him, "Who is he, O Allâh's Messenger?" He replied, "The person whose neighbor is not safe from his injurious conduct." (*Al-Bukhârî* and *Muslim*)

"He is not a [true] believer who eats his fill when his neighbor beside him is hungry." (*Mishkat Al-Masâbîh*)

"To Allâh, the best friends are those who are best to each other, and the best neighbors are those who are best to each other." (*At-Tirmidhî*)

"Angel Gabriel kept exhorting me about the [good treatment of] the neighbor to the point that I thought he would grant him the right of inheritance." (*Al-Bukhârî*)

Being Dutiful to the Parents

Islam commands kindness and righteousness towards the parents and considers this noble trait next to the worship of God. The Qur'ân says:

"And We have enjoined upon man to be good and dutiful to his parents." (29:8)

"And your Lord has decreed that you worship none but Him, and that you be dutiful to your parents. If one of them or both of them attain old age in your life, say not to them a word of disrespect, nor shout at them, but address them in terms of honor. And lower unto them the wing of submission and humility through mercy, and say: 'My Lord! Bestow upon them Your Mercy as

they did bring me up when I was young.'" (17:23, 24)

"And We have enjoined on man [to be dutiful and good] to his parents. In travail upon travail did his mother bear him; and in two years was his weaning; [hear the command:] 'Show gratitude to Me and to your parents, to Me is your [final] goal.'" (31:14)

The Prophet 鑿 says:

"Paradise is at the feet of mothers." (*An-Nasâ'î*)

A person once came to the Prophet 鑿 and sought his permission to participate in *Jihâd* [fighting or struggling in Allâh's way]. The Prophet 鑿 asked him, "Are your parents still alive?" The man replied in the affirmative. The Prophet 鑿 then said, "[You should] consider their service as *Jihâd.*" (*Al-Bukhârî* and *Muslim*)

Respecting the Elderly and showing Affection towards the Women and the Young

Islam commands Muslims to respect the elderly and to show affection and mercy towards children. The Prophet 鑿 says:

"There is none amongst us who does not show mercy towards the young ones and respect and honor the elderly." (*At-Tirmidhî*)

It happened once that the Prophet 鑿 kissed his grandson Al-Hasan in the presence of Al-Aqra' bin Aâbis. When the latter saw this he remarked: "I have

Commands for the Good

ten children and I have never kissed any one of them."
The Prophet ﷺ looked at him and said: "He who does
not show mercy towards others, [Allâh] will not show
mercy towards him." (*Al-Bukhârî* and *Muslim*)

The leader of congregational prayer is commanded to make
the prayer a little bit shorter in consideration of those who are
behind him. The Prophet ﷺ said:

> "If any one of you leads the prayer, you should make it
> a bit shorter, for the congregation includes the infirm,
> the ill and the aged. If, however, you are offering
> prayer alone, then you can lengthen it as much as you
> wish." (*Al-Bukhârî* and *Muslim*)

Even in time of war, Islam commands its fighters to show
kindness towards women, children, the elderly and the
infirm. The Prophet ﷺ used to instruct Muslim soldiers when
they were heading for the battlefield thus:

> "Do not kill any old person, any child or any woman."
> (*Abu Dâwûd*)

> "Do not kill the monks in monasteries." (*Ibn Hanbal*)

> "Do not kill the people who are sitting in a place of
> worship." (*Musnad Ibn Hanbal*)

> "Do not kill a wounded person, nor chase a fleeing
> person, nor kill a captive."

Helping the Needy

Islam urges Muslims to extend a helping hand to the needy

Commands for the Good

and make the afflicted happy. The Prophet ﷺ says:

"A Muslim is the brother of a Muslim. He neither oppresses him, nor does he fail him. He who relieves a Muslim of an affliction, Allâh will relieve him of one of the afflictions of the Day of Judgment. He who covers a Muslim's faults, Allâh will cover his own faults on the Day of Judgment." (*Muslim*)

Islam encourages Muslims to show mercy towards those in straitened circumstances and to grant them a respite until they have enough to repay their debts, or forgo the amount in case of the borrower's hardship. The Qur'ân says:

"If the debtor is in a difficulty, grant him time till it is easy for him to repay. But if you remit it by way of charity, that is best for you if you only knew." (2:280)

The Prophet ﷺ says:

"There was a merchant who used to advance money to people. If he realized there was a debtor amongst his clients who was in a difficulty, he would tell his servants: 'Do not take anything from him; forgive him so that Allâh may forgive us'. And so Allâh forgave his sins." (*Al-Bukhârî*)

Mercy towards the Animals

Islam commands its followers to show mercy not only towards human beings but also towards animals. A person who ill-treats animals is regarded in Islam as a sinner and will

Commands for the Good

consequently invite Allâh's wrath. The Prophet ﷺ says:

> "A women was punished in Hell on account of a cat which she had confined until death. She neither gave it to eat or to drink when she confined it, nor did she set it free so that it might eat the vermin of the earth." (*Al-Bukhârî* and *Muslim*)

> "A man approached a well, descended inside it and drank to his fill. Outside the well there happened to be a dog that was panting out of extreme thirst. The man felt mercy towards it. So he took off one of his shoes, filled it with water and handed it to the dog to quench its thirst. Allâh was pleased with the man's good deed and admitted him into Paradise." (*Al-Bukhârî* and *Muslim*)

> It happened once that a donkey with a brand on its face happened to pass before the Prophet ﷺ. Upon seeing the brand he said: "May Allâh curse him who has branded it." (*Muslim*)

Another narration states:

> Allâh's Messenger ﷺ prohibited us from hitting across the face and branding [animals] on the face." (*Muslim*)

Islam also gives clear-cut instructions as to the proper manner of killing an animal for food. The Prophet ﷺ says:

> "Allâh has prescribed excellence and perfection in everything. So if you intend to kill [an animal], do so in the best possible manner; and if you intend to slaughter

[an animal], do so in the best possible manner. Let everyone of you properly sharpen his knife and give ease to the animal." (*Muslim*)

Strengthening One Another

Islam calls to unity and harmony and exhorts against discord and hatred. The Qur'ân says:

"And hold fast, all together, to the Rope of Allâh [i.e., this Qur'ân] and be not divided." (3:103)

It also calls its followers to reciprocate love, affection, honesty and co-operation with one another. The Prophet ﷺ says:

"The bonds of brotherhood between two believers are like [the bricks] of a building, each one of which supports and strengthens the other." (*Al-Bukhârî*)

"The believers in their mutual kindness, compassion and sympathy are just like one body. When one of the limbs is afflicted, the whole body responds with wakefulness and fever." (*Al-Bukhârî* and *Muslim*)

Forgiving Others' Offences

Islam invites its followers to overlook other people's offences:

"Let them forgive and pass over [the offence]. Do you not desire that Allâh should forgive you?" (24:22)

Commands for the Good

"Repel evil with that which is best." (23:96)

Honoring the Covenants

Islam also commands its followers to honor their covenants and fulfil all their obligations:

"O you who believe! Fulfil [all] obligations." (5:1)

It strongly condemns betrayal and treachery:

"And fulfil the covenant; for the covenant shall be questioned about." (17:34)

The Prophet ﷺ says:

"For everyone who breaks his covenant, there will be a flag on the Day of Judgment, and it will be said [to his or her humiliation before all creation]: 'This is [proof of] betrayal by so-and-so.'" (*Muslim*)

"Allâh the Almighty said: 'I will contend against three [types of] people on the Day of Judgment: A person who has made a covenant in My Name and then has broken it; a person who has sold a free man and then has devoured his price; and a person who has hired a laborer and has not given him his pay after he has obtained his due in full from him.'" (*Al-Bukhârî*).

Islam considers disloyalty an act of hypocrisy, which entails Allâh's wrath and punishment in the Hereafter. The

Prophet ﷺ says:

> "Whoever possesses these four characteristics is a hypocrite; and anyone who possesses one of them in fact possesses a trait of hypocrisy until he gives it up: when he is entrusted [with something], he proves dishonest; when he speaks, he tells lies; when he makes a covenant, he breaks it; and when he quarrels, he behaves in a very impudent, insulting manner." (*Al-Bukhârî* and *Muslim*)

Reconciliation at the Time of Conflicts

Islam encourages its followers to adjust all matters of difference and settle disputes to pave the way for a peaceful, harmonious society. It also calls them to reconcile between the conflicting parties:

> "The believers are nothing else than brothers. So make reconciliation between your brothers." (49:10)

> "So fear Allâh and adjust all matters of difference among you." (8:1)

The Prophet ﷺ says:

> "To reconcile two people is [an act of] charity." (*Al-Bukhârî* and *Muslim*)

Commands for the Good

Enjoining Good and Forbidding Evil

Enjoining virtue and forbidding evil plays a vital part in the reformation of society at large and is a very effective tool for the eradication of evil. Islam urges its followers to spare no pains to fulfil their obligations and help one another to stand by the truth in patience and unshaken constancy in the midst of corruption, decadence and spiritual stagnation. The Qur'ân says:

> "And let there arise out of you a band of people inviting to all that is good, enjoining what is right, and forbidding what is wrong: they are the ones to attain felicity." (3: 104)

The Prophet ﷺ says:

> "Whoever invites [people] to a [form of] guidance, will have its reward as well as the reward of [all] those who act upon it without anything diminished from their rewards; and whoever invites to an evil [thing], will shoulder its sin as well as the sins of [all] those who act upon it without diminishing the burden of these sins in the least." (*Muslim*)

> "He who guides to [a form of] virtue will have the same reward as that of those who act upon it." (*Muslim*)

Commands for the Good

The Qur'ân commends the Muslim community for its observance of this noble trait:

"You are the best of people raised for the good of mankind: you enjoin what is right, forbid what is wrong and believe in Allâh." (3:110)

If these Divine commands are neglected, evil will without a shadow of doubt prevail and both the upright and the crooked will be doomed to Allâh's wrath. The Qur'ân says about 'the Children of Israel':

"Those amongst the Children of Israel who disbelieved were cursed by the tongue of David and Jesus, son of Mary. That was because they disobeyed and persisted in excesses. They did not forbid one another the inequities which they committed. Evil indeed was that which they did." (5:78-9)

The Prophet ﷺ sets forth a very beautiful parable about this:

"The analogy of those who observe Allâh's set limits and those who transgress them is similar to that of a group of people who get on board a ship after casting lots. Some of them are in the upper deck and some of them in the lower deck When those in the lower deck require water they go to those in the upper deck and say [to them]: 'Could we make a hole without causing harm to the group in the upper deck?' If those in the upper deck allow them to carry out their design, they will all perish; but if they do not allow them to do so,

they will all be saved." (*Al-Bukhârî*)

Islam commands Muslims to observe these Divine commands to the best of their ability. The Prophet ﷺ says:

"Whoever of you sees something wrong, he must change it with his hand [i.e., by action or deed); if he cannot, let him try to change it with his tongue; if he cannot, then let him try to change it with his heart [i.e., by showing feelings of disapproval and condemnation], and this is the minimal degree of Faith." (*Muslim*)

Ascertaining the Correctness of Reports

Another noteworthy beauty of Islam is that it commands its followers to ascertain the correctness of reports lest they should do injustice to others:

"O you who believe! If an evil person [or liar] comes to you with any news, verify it lest you should harm people unwittingly, and then become regretful for what you have done." (49:6)

"And follow not [i.e., say not, or do not, or witness not, etc.] that of which you have no knowledge [e.g., one's saying ' I have seen' while in fact he has not seen anything, or 'I have heard' while in fact he has not heard anything]. Verily, the hearing, the sight and the heart – all these shall be called to account." (17:36)

Character at its Best

Islam calls to be of noble character and rewards abundantly

Commands for the Good

those who observe it. The Prophet ﷺ says:

> "The believers with perfect Faith are those whose character is the best, and the best amongst you are those who are best to their wives." (*At-Tirmidhî*)

The Prophet ﷺ says:

> "The believer can attain the rank of those who offer nocturnal supererogatory prayers and observe supererogatory fasts, as a result of his good character." (*Abu Dâwûd*)

> "The dearest and nearest amongst you to me on the Day of Judgment are those with the best character, and the most abhorrent to me and the farthest from me on the Day of Judgment are the pompous, boastful, braggarts and the arrogant people." (*At-Tirmidhî*)

It seems that the Prophet ﷺ was sent only to complete the most noble character traits. As he said:

> "Surely, I was only sent to complete the most noble character traits." (*Al-Bukhârî*)

All the religious obligations such as prayer, fasting and pilgrimage are meant to nurture good character. The Qur'ân says:

> "For *Hajj* are the months well-known. If anyone undertakes that duty therein, let there be no obscenity, nor wickedness, nor wrangling in the *Hajj*. And whatever good you do, [be sure] Allâh knows it. And

Commands for the Good

take a provision [with you] for the journey, but the best of provisions is right conduct." (2:197)

"Recite what is sent of the Book by inspiration to you, and establish regular prayer: for prayer restrains from shameful and evil deeds." (29:45)

The Prophet ﷺ says:

"If one of you is fasting, he should not use obscene language or behave foolishly and impudently; and if someone fights with him or abuses him, he should say: 'I am fasting! I am fasting!'" (*Al-Bukhârî* and *Muslim*)

"Whoever does not abstain from deceitful speech and actions [while fasting], Allâh is not in need of him leaving his food and drink." (*Al-Bukhârî*)

Generosity will be repaid

The Qur'ân says:

"And whatever you spend in good, it is for yourselves, when you spend not except seeking Allâh's Countenance; and whatsoever good thing you spend, it will be repaid to you in full, and you will not be wronged." (2: 272)

"And whatever you spend in good, surely Allâh knows it well." (2:273)

A man asked the Prophet ﷺ: "Which act in Islam is the best?" He replied, "To feed [the needy] and to greet

Commands for the Good

everyone, whether you know them or not." (*Al-Bukhârî* and *Muslim*)

Jâbir ﷺ, one of the Prophet's Companions, said, "Allâh's Messenger ﷺ never said 'no' to anyone who asked him for anything." (*Al-Bukhârî* and *Muslim*)

Loving for Others what One loves for Oneself

Islam urges its followers to desire for others what they desire for themselves, and to treat them in the same manner they like to be treated. The Qur'ân says about the true believers:

"And [they] give preference over themselves, even though poverty was their [own lot]." (59:9)

The Prophet ﷺ says:

"None of you will be considered a true believer until he loves for his brother what he loves for himself." (*Al-Bukhârî*)

The Prophet ﷺ says:

"A slave will not attain [the state of] perfect Faith until he enjoys three characteristics: spending [in the way of Allâh] in time of poverty, treating others with justice even though it may be against himself, and giving currency to the greeting of peace [i.e., *As-Salamu 'Alaikum*]."

"Whoever has more than one mount should offer it to him who does not have any; whoever has surplus food

Commands for the Good

should give it to him who has nothing." (*Muslim*)

The narrator of this tradition said that the Prophet ﷺ went on specifying all sorts of provision until we thought that none of us had any right whatsoever to any surplus things we had.

Defending the Honor of Others

Islam makes it an obligation upon every Muslim to defend his brother's honor, property and blood, in their absence, as much as he can. Abud-Darda' ﷺ, the renowned *Hadith* narrator, reported that a man abused another man in his absence and another man who was then present defended the latter. To this the Prophet ﷺ, who was also a witness to the incident, said:

> "He who defends his brother's honor, Allâh will keep away Hellfire from [burning] his face [on the Day of Judgment]." (*At-Tirmidhî*)

The Great Merit and Reward of Patience

Islam prompts its followers to observe patience and perseverance in three ways: patience and steadfastness while acting upon Allâh's commands, patience while striving hard to avoid Allâh's prohibitions, and patience when afflicted with calamity.

Patience here implies a number of things including patience in the sense of being thorough not hasty. To have patience, perseverance, constancy, steadfastness, firmness of purpose and a cheerful attitude of resignation in sorrow or suffering as opposed to murmuring or rebellion. To be patient and

overcome passivity and listlessness with constancy and steadfastness.

Patience and *Salât* [prayer] are extremely helpful tools in times of calamity and distress. The Qur'ân says:

"And seek Allâh's help with patient perseverance and *Salât* [prayer]." (2:45)

Patience in Islam has an extremely great merit and its reward with Allâh is boundless. The Qur'ân says:

"And be steadfast in patience; for verily Allâh will not suffer the reward of the righteous to perish." (11:115)

"If you persevere patiently and observe piety, - then that indeed is a matter of great resolution." (3:186)

Hygiene in all Aspects of Life

A closer look at the teachings of Islam will reveal that it calls to hygiene in all aspects of life.

Islam commands its followers to use their right hands while eating or drinking because the left hand is solely reserved for such things as cleaning oneself in the bathroom after answering the call of nature. This excellent habit makes one aware at all times which hand to utilize on which occasion.

Islam prohibits certain foods for the sake of hygiene. The Qur'ân says:

"He [i.e., Allâh] has only forbidden you dead meat and blood and the flesh of the swine, and that on which any other name has been invoked besides that of Allâh."

(2:173)

"Forbidden to you [for food] are: dead meat, blood, the flesh of swine, and that on which Allâh's Name has not been invoked, that which has been killed by strangling, or by a violent blow, or by a headlong fall, or by being gored to death, that which has been partly eaten by a wild animal unless you are able to slaughter it [in due form before is death]..." (5:3)

If an animal dies as a result of strangling or a violent blow or a headlong fall or by being gored to death, or by being attacked by a wild animal, the presumption is that it becomes carrion, as the lifeblood is congealed before being taken out of the body.

However, if the lifeblood still flows and the solemn mode of slaughter in the Name of Allâh is carried out, it becomes lawful as food.

Carrion or dead meat and blood as articles of food are naturally repulsive. Pork has more fat than muscle-building material, the first meat any cardiologist, from among people who eat swine, tells the patient to stop eating is pork. It is more liable to disease than other kinds of meat, e.g., trichinosis, characterized by hair-like worms in the muscular tissue. [1]

Cleanliness is not only "next to godliness" but also "half the Faith", as the Prophet ﷺ clearly states. Prayer will not be valid without *Wudhu'* [ablution]. Ablutions require the washing of those parts of the body that are generally exposed to dirt or dust, such as the face, the arms and the feet.

1   See Yusuf Ali, *The Holy Qur'ân: English Translation of the Meanings & Commentary,*1990, p.69.

Ablutions become nullified as a result of responding to the call of nature, sleep, and sexual activity, etc. The *Ghusl* [bath] requires the washing of the whole body after wet dreams, sexual intercourse, upon expiration of the menstruation period for women and at the end of postnatal bleeding, which is estimated at a maximum of forty days. The importance and beneficial results of cleanliness on Muslims is crystal clear if we remember that they have to perform ablution before their prayers. Allâh loves those who observe cleanliness:

> "Allâh loves those who turn to Him constantly and He loves those who keep themselves pure and clean." (2:222)

Commands for the Good

Prohibitions of the Bad

Fornication and Adultery

Islam prohibits fornication, adultery, and all the unlawful acts that are bound to lead to it, such as lustful looks and private meetings. It has ordained the stoning of adulterers and adulteresses, the whipping of fornicators and the killing of homosexuals publicly with a view to safeguarding people's honor, upholding moral values, encouraging decency and chastity and protecting society at large against moral deterioration and ultimate ruin.

With regard to this issue, the well-known saying, "Prevention is better than cure" finds full scope in Islam. For Islam takes all the necessary preventive measures to guard against the degeneration of moral values in the Muslim society. The Qur'ân considers any act leading to abominable deeds forbidden. The Qur'ân says:

> "And come not near to adultery; for it is an indecent deed and an evil way." (17:32)

Commenting upon this Verse, Yusuf Ali writes:

> "Adultery is not only shameful in itself and inconsistent with any self-respect or respect for others, but it opens the road to many evils. It destroys the basis

of the family: it works against the interests of children born or to be born; it may cause murders and feuds and loss of reputation and property, and also loosens permanently the bonds of society. Nor only should it be avoided as a sin, but any approach or temptation to it should be avoided." [1]

Usury

Islam forbids usury in the strongest possible terms due to the numerous social ills it is bound to trigger. Usurious transactions, in the Islamic value system, represent a prominent source of unjustified advantage. The Qur'ân forbids its followers to acquire each other's property wrongfully:

"And eat up not one another's property unjustly, nor give bribery to the judges [before presenting your case] that you may eat up a part of the property of others sinfully." (2:188)

Usury represents the highest form of eating up others' property unlawfully. It is "not only a source of great injustice but also of misallocation of resources, erratic growth, economic instability and a number of other economic problems." [2]

Prohibitions of the Bad

---

[1] Yousuf Ali, *The Holy Qur'ân: English Translation of the Meanings and Commentary,* King Fahd Holy Qur'ân Printing Complex, 1990, pp. 785-6.

[2] M.Umar Chapra, *Towards a Just Monetary System,* The Islamic Foundation, 1985, p. 56.

Islam aims to establish justice and eradicate exploitation in all its forms. Usurious transactions also spoil human relations due to the harm they incur upon debtors. They also give rise to a group of non-productive people who are no benefit to their society. Whereas legitimate trade or industry, which the Qur'ân commends and encourages, increases the prosperity and the stability of men and nations. A dependence on usury definitely encourages a culture of fruitless, cruel parasites and selfish people who will do more harm to their societies than good. The Qur'ân says:

"Those who eat usury will not stand except as stands one whom the Satan by his touch has driven to madness. That is because they say, 'Trade is like usury,' but Allâh has permitted trade and forbidden usury. Those who, after receiving admonition from their Lord, desist shall be pardoned for the past; their case is for Allâh [to judge]; but those who repeat [the offence] are dwellers of the Fire: they will abide therein." (2:275)

"Allâh will deprive usury of all blessing, but will give increase for deeds of charity: for Allâh loves not any ungrateful sinner." (2:276)

"O you who believe! Fear Allâh and give up what remains of your demand for usury, if you are indeed believers. If you do it not, take notice of war from Allâh and His Messenger, but if you repent, you shall

have your capital sums: Deal not unjustly, and you shall not be dealt with unjustly." (2:278-9)

Alcoholic Beverages

Islam prohibits all sorts of alcoholic beverages and labels them "the root of all evil" on account of the evil they cause. The Qur'ân says:

"O you who believe! Intoxicants and gambling, sacrificing to stones, and [divination by] arrows, are abominations of Satan's handiwork: Eschew such [abominations] that you may prosper." (5:90)

By prohibiting all sort of intoxicants, Islam aims at creating a responsible and reliable society free of dependencies. It wants all the individuals in the society to keep their sobriety and soundness of mind, safeguard their property from unnecessary and exorbitant expenses and protect their purity and good character.

Those addicted to such contemptible beverages are to be first of all requested to repent. If they persist in their evil actions, which affect society negatively, they will then be subjected to the punishment of a public whipping, which serves as a deterrent to all.

Immoral Behavior

Islam makes it utterly forbidden for men to ape women and vice versa, in either appearance or conduct. For imitation of

Prohibitions of the Bad

the opposite sex in dress, movements or the way of speaking is undoubtedly a manifest diversion from what is right and natural. Tolerance of such forms of perversion in the name of civilization and progress, in many societies has triggered numerous social, moral, and physical diseases.

Islam wants its followers to adhere to the noble principles dictated by its pure nature. For man is created a Muslim, in other words innocent, pure, true and inclined to right and virtue. It is the network of perversion prevalent in the environment into which one is born that affects this natural purity of Islam and turns one away from it, making one unclean, false, and desiring for what is wrong and harmful. It deflects one from the worship of the One True God. The Prophet ﷺ says:

> "Every child is born on the *Fitrah*, or in a pure state of nature [i.e., Muslim]. It is his parents who convert him to Judaism, Christianity or Magianism. Read, if so you will, the Verse: 'So set your face truly to the religion of pure Islamic monotheism, the nature in which Allâh has created mankind: No change let there be in the religion of Allâh. That is the straight religion, but most among mankind know not.' (30:30)"

Islam came to cure this crookedness and to restore human nature to its right and original course.

Avoidance of Things not Relevant

A Muslim should not engage in something, which does not concern him. The Prophet ﷺ says:

"A sign of a person's good Faith is that he does not engage in that which does not benefit him." (*At-Tirmidhi*).

Many Muslims, however, seem to have neglected the instruction underlying this beautiful saying. Were they to act upon this *Hadith,* they would certainly avoid many problems, disputes and arguments.

Severing of Blood Relationship

Another beautiful aspect of Islam is that it strictly prohibits the severing of the ties of blood relationship. The Qur'ân says:

"And fear Allâh through whom you demand your mutual [rights], and [do not sever the relations of] the wombs [i.e., kinship]." (4:1)

The Prophet ﷺ says in this connection:

"The person who severs the bonds of kinship will not enter Paradise." (*Al-Bukhârî*)

"He who believes in Allâh and the Last Day, must join the ties of relationship" (*Al-Bukhârî* and *Muslim*).

Other Social Vices

Islam also prohibits backbiting, calumny, spying, lying, betrayal and all such ignoble traits. There are numerous references to these in the Qur'ân and the *Sunnah* [the traditions of the Prophet ﷺ]. Here are a few of them.

The Qur'ân says:

"O you who believe! Let not some men among you deride other men: it may be that the latter are better than the former; nor let women deride other women: it may be the latter are better than the former; nor defame one another, nor insult one another by nicknames. Bad indeed is an evil reputation after the profession of Faith; and those who repent not are the wrongdoers. O you who believe! Avoid suspicion as much [as possible]; for suspicion in some cases is a sin. And spy not, nor backbite one another. Would any of you like to eat the flesh of his dead [Muslim] brother? Certainly, you would loathe it. And fear Allâh. Surely, Allâh is Oft-Returning, Merciful." (49:11, 12)

"Verily, Allâh commands you to render back the trusts to those entitled to them." (4:58)

"Do not help one another in sin and transgression." (5:2)

The Prophet ﷺ says:

"Do not desert one another, do not nurse hatred towards one another, do not be jealous of one another, and be, O slaves of Allâh, true brothers. It is not lawful for a Muslim to give up talking to his [Muslim] brother for more than three days." (*Al-Bukhârî* and *Muslim*)

"The person who goes about with calumnies will not enter Paradise." (*Al-Bukhârî* and *Muslim*)

Prohibitions of the Bad

"It is enough for a man to prove himself a liar when he goes on narrating whatever he hears." (*Muslim*)

"A [true] Muslim is one from whose tongue Muslims are safe." (*Al-Bukhârî* and *Muslim*)

"Beware of envy, because envy destroys virtues just as the fire destroys the firewood." (*Abu Dâwûd*)

"Beware of suspicion, for suspicion is the worst of false tales." (*Al-Bukhârî* and *Muslim*)

"It is enough evil for a Muslim to look down upon his [Muslim] brother." (*Muslim*)

Prohibitions of the Bad

Conclusion

These are a few examples of the beauty of Islam. Islam liberated the ignorant, ruthless Arabs from oppressing one another, united their ranks, refined their manners, delivered them from evil, turned them into a civilized and cultivated nation after they had been torn with civil and tribal feuds and dissension. When they dedicated themselves completely to the Truth and stood by it, their empire was born in a matter of a few years and Islam reigned supreme everywhere. The Qur'ân says:

> "And remember with gratitude Allâh's Favor on you; for you were enemies and He joined your hearts in love, so that by His Grace, you became brothers. And you were on the brink of the pit of Fire, and He saved you from it. Thus does Allâh make His signs clear to you, that you may be guided." (3:103)

> "Call to mind when you were a small [band], deemed weak through the land, and afraid that men might despoil and kidnap you; but he provided a safe place for you, strengthened you with His aid, and gave you good things for sustenance, that you might be grateful." (8:26)

Islam's enemies get closer to it and embrace it wittingly or unwittingly because it is the truth from Allâh. Their inventions, science and technology only serve to testify that Islam is beyond any shadow of doubt a true religion. The Qur'ân says:

> "Soon will We show them Our signs in the universe and in themselves, until it becomes manifest to them that this is the truth. Is it not enough that your Lord does witness all things?" (41:53)

Being the true religion from Allâh, Islam will never wane despite the all-out attacks leveled against it. Its Divine light will continue to illuminate people's hearts and souls, deliver them from evil, and spread justice and mercy. The Qur'ân says:

> "Their intention is to extinguish Allâh's Light with their mouths! But Allâh will complete His Light even though the disbelievers may detest [it]." (61:8)

Conclusion

The Qur'ân draws a clear distinction between the dead and the living:

> "So verily you cannot make the dead [i.e., the disbelievers] to hear, nor can you make the deaf to hear the call, when they show their backs and turn away. Nor can you lead back the blind from their straying. You can make to hear only those who believe in Our signs and submit [their will to Islam]." (30:52-3)

> "Can he, who was dead [as a result of his disbelief] and We gave him life [Faith] and made for him a light whereby he walks among men, be like him who is in the depths darkness [of disbelief] whence he cannot come out?" (6:122)

The marvels of Allâh's creation can be realized in a general way by everyone who has an inclination to allow such knowledge to penetrate his mind. But if men, out of perversity, kill the very faculty, which Allâh has given them, how can they then understand? How can the truth reach such people who turn their backs and stubbornly refuse to be instructed at all? Though they have seemingly all the faculties of reason and perception, they have so deadened them that those faculties do not function, and they go headlong into Hell:

> "Many are the jinn and mankind for Hell: they have hearts wherewith they understand not, eyes wherewith they see not, and ears wherewith they hear not,– nay even more astray. They are the heedless ones." (7:179)

Conclusion